Ad-n

Ad-mission

The Briefing and Debriefing of Teams of Missionaries and Aid Workers

Graham Fawcett

First Published in Great Britain 1999
Graham Fawcett
Youth With A Mission
Highfield Oval
Harpenden, Herts
AL5 4BX
gfawcett@oval.com

Copyright © Graham Fawcett 1999

The right of Graham Fawcett to be identified as the author of this work has been asserted by him in accordance with the Copyright, Designs and Patents Act 1988

ISBN 0 9535845 0 X

Reprinted 2000

All rights reserved. No part of this book may be reproduced or transmitted in any form or by any means, electronic or mechanical, including photocopying, recording or by any information storage and retrieval system, without permission in writing from the author.

Quotations are taken from the following sources.
All rights reserved:

APA (1994) *DSM III-R and DSM-IV*, Washington, American Psychiatric Association for the tables in Chapter 6.

Davidson, S., *The People In Aid Code of Best Practice*, Relief and Rehabilitation Network Paper 20, London, 1997 for the reproduction of the summary of recommendations in Appendix 6.

John Paul II, *Crossing the Threshold of Hope*, London, Jonathan Cape, 1994 for quotes in Chapter 7.

Nouwen H, McNeill, D., and Morrison D.A., *Compassion*, London, Darton, Longman, Todd. 1982 for quotes in Chapter 2.

Scripture quotations taken from the
HOLY BIBLE, NEW INTERNATIONAL VERSION.
Copyright 1973, 1978, 1984 by International Bible Society.
Used by permission of Hodder and Stoughton Ltd, a member of the Hodder Headline Plc Group. All rights reserved. 'NIV' is a trademark of the International Bible Society.
UK trademark number 1448790.

Typeset by Dorchester Typesetting Group Ltd, Dorchester
Printed in Great Britain by Athenaeum Press Ltd, Gateshead

Contents

Introduction ix

Chapter 1	Briefing and debriefing – why now?	1
Chapter 2	Common challenges in the selection process	7
Chapter 3	Briefing	19
Chapter 4	Routine Debriefing	61
Chapter 5	Training debriefers	99
Chapter 6	Post Traumatic Stress Disorder	107
Chapter 7	Suffering	121
Appendix 1	Routine re-entry simulations for training debriefers	139
Appendix 2	Training simulators	141
Appendix 3	Pastoral visits	145
Appendix 4	Career interviews	149
Appendix 5	Notes on Missionary Kids	155
Appendix 6	Summary of the Macnair report	159
Appendix 7	PIA best practice summary	161

Preface

This gem of a book is a one-stop shopping source for your briefing and debriefing needs. Graham's years of experience as a psychologist and in missionary care really show. This is a how-to book, rich with insights and resources and full of practical suggestions that can be applied to various mission settings. Written in the current member care context of developing "best practice guidelines", it will be of much help to agency leaders, personnel managers, cross-cultural trainers, mental health professionals and all those with member care responsibilities. The additional sections on selection, training debriefers, PTSD, suffering and several appendices are a real bonus. Thank you Graham for your timely and substantial contribution to the member care field.

Dr Kelly O'Donnell
Coordinator,
Member Care Task Force, World Evangelical Fellowship's Mission Commission

Acknowledgements

Heather Wright – Many of the ideas and detailed working through of the concepts in this book are due to her insistence on getting things right rather than merely adequate. Thank you Heather as well for detailed comments on the first rough draft of the book, for many helpful comments and discussions over the six years we worked together and for encouraging the writing of the book in the first place.

Lynn Green, Debbie Lovell, Kelly O'Donnell, Christine Sine and Patty Timbrell – for working hard to offer such helpful comments and criticisms of the various drafts.

Some 700 students, returned missionaries and volunteers who have been such willing participants in my efforts to help them make sense of their experiences.

Many in YWAM and other agencies, particularly David, Janet, Jackie, Sandy and Sue, who have nagged me and cajoled me to write things down.

Ken Ruskin of KR Production Services and Consultancy for helping to get the book to the market place.

Janet and Samuel who have seen rather less of me than they otherwise might.

And, particularly:

S, A and R. The three returnees I feel I have failed the most and yet who graciously stuck with me over several years and freely shared their anger, frustration and hurts. They are the benchmark against which this work has to stand. To them this book is dedicated – may your stories never be repeated.

Introduction

I sat in silence, dumb struck at the information I had just received from an embassy official in an Eastern European nation in 1991. 80% of referrals to the local embassy clinics were for psychiatric reasons, mainly depression, anxiety and psychosomatic complaints. Careful monitoring revealed that particular aid agencies were over represented. Those agencies neither adequately selected nor supported their field staff. The same pattern was being repeated throughout the rest of Eastern Europe. The joint response of the diplomatic corps was brief and to the point – they were considering giving the national government a short list of those agencies who seemed to be behaving irresponsibly and respectfully suggesting that entry visas be denied to their workers.

For me the choice was clear – to stay in the country working where so many others were already doing an excellent job or return to the UK and try to influence the way in which people are chosen and equipped for the field.

This book is a result of that conversation and my choice to work full time within the UK.

Over the years people have asked me to document the work and rationale of Youth With A Mission's (YWAM) approach to briefing and debriefing in the United Kingdom so that the work may be multiplied. I have tried for some time to do that and I hope that the result is of help to those who seek to prepare overseas missionaries and aid workers.

Increasingly missionaries and aid workers find themselves in difficult circumstances overseas. War zones, famine areas, refugee camps and people experiencing extreme poverty are all situations that people working abroad increasingly face. Some workers face these issues for a few weeks, others for years. All need training to ensure they do more than simply survive in the situations they go to.

The publication of a number of initiatives in the UK have been timely. The Macnair report[1] published in the wake of the tragedy of Rwanda emphasised both the absence of and the need for adequate care of aid workers in particular. The UK government and NGO initiative, People In Aid,[2] has sought to put into practice the recommendations of the Macnair report. A concurrent initiative by the British Evangelical Missionary Alliance and the British Evangelical Alliance[3] has sought to do the same for short term missionaries in Christian agencies. YWAM internationally has recently adopted its own Codes of Best Practice relating to training and debriefing.[4]

We in YWAM(UK) have been working towards ensuring that people going to serve overseas are equipped for the work God has called them to do. Our aim is to ensure that the right people are selected and that those selected are adequately prepared. On return we then ensure they are adequately debriefed. For a small number more extensive debriefing is necessary. In all of this we seek to extend the Kingdom of God.

Graham Fawcett
Easter 1999

---

[1] Macnair, R., *Room For Improvement: The Management and Support of Relief and Development Workers. Network Paper 10*, Relief and Rehabilitation Network, London, Overseas Development Institute, 1995. (See Appendix 6).

[2] Davidson, S., *The People In Aid Code of Best Practice in the Management and Support of Aid Personnel. Network Paper 20*, Relief and Rehabilitation Network, London, Overseas Development Institute, 1997. (See Appendix 7).

[3] *UK Evangelical Missionary Alliance/Evangelical Alliance Code of Best Practice in Short Term Mission.* London, Unpublished Document launched June 1997.

[4] Available on the Web at www.angelfire.com/ak/ywammmi

Chapter 1

Briefing and Debriefing – Why Now?

The psychiatric consequences for aid workers in Rwanda and Romania, coupled with the publication of the Macnair report in the UK, have been major factors in the increasing awareness of the need for adequate pastoral care of workers who go abroad. It is no longer ethically or morally acceptable to send aid workers or missionaries abroad unprepared for the realities of what they are likely to encounter. It is also no longer acceptable to send people into situations which it is probable they will be unable to deal with. It can only be a matter of time before civil litigation is used against those who fail in their 'duty of care'.[1]

Perhaps ironically, from a Christian perspective, it is the Military who have excelled in preparing people for traumatic situations and helping them deal with the consequences of those situations.[2] It is no coincidence that it was a military psychiatrist (Gordon Turnbull) who debriefed civilians such as Terry Waite following their difficult overseas experiences. Whilst valuable military intelligence was to be gathered from them there were also few non-military mental health professionals available at the time with the necessary skills.

The briefing and debriefing of civilian emergency workers and the debriefing of civilians caught up in traumatic situations has become standard practice but the application of this knowledge to aid workers and missionaries is sparse. A number of publications have been available concerning missionary preparation and care in general[3,4,5,6] but the translation of theory into practice has been broadly lacking. The very terms 'briefing' and 'debriefing' are themselves military terms and were originally sessions where military personnel would be given factual information concerning their mission and then asked for detailed factual information on their return.

The psychiatric phenomena now known as Post Traumatic Stress Disorder (PTSD) has also provided a civilian and military focus in this area and much work has now been conducted in the area of PTSD arising from military service. More recently, researchers have turned their attention to the phenomena of PTSD in the civilian population and have used two focii. The first has been the effect of disasters such as major accidents or major natural disasters on civilians. The second has been the effect of attending such disasters on civilian emergency service personnel. The phenomena of

PTSD and stressors generally in aid workers or other ex-patriate workers such as missionaries has not been studied in any significant detail until recently. [7,8]

Clearly missionaries and aid workers experience a variety of stressors other than the dramatic ones associated with trauma. Some of them are the normal stresses associated with re-locating a home or family, entering a new culture, working within that culture and then the, often unexpected, shock of re-entering one's supposedly safe home culture. Common reactions include mourning the life that has been left behind and feelings of profound isolation on return home. Other stressors are more severe but less universal. They may be the more potent for being unexpected. Missionaries and development workers evacuated from Rwanda and, currently, Zaire could not possibly have anticipated the enormity of what they were to face.

Given the wealth of literature and codes of conduct now available it is clear that responsible agencies now have all the necessary knowledge available to prepare their workers well for overseas service. Both the expected stress of entry and re-entry adjustments together with the possibility of coping with more extreme stressors can be prepared for. The task requires effort but is not onerous.

There are a number of factors involved. Rigorous selection against established requirements, much of which can be a paper exercise, is essential given the numbers applying for less than helpful reasons. Many people are attracted by the apparent glamour of relief work. Others may be driven by guilt arising from media coverage of events overseas and so feel they must help. Still others want to help but feel inadequate. All candidates for our programmes are sent a detailed application form. References are taken up from people who know the candidate well and from their church. A medical evaluation is also carried out. For longer term programmes we may have a selection weekend which mainly consists of outlining the cost and challenge of service overseas.

At this point four inter-related sets of support may be offered or required by an agency for its staff about to embark on overseas work. These are briefing prior to departure, orientation on arrival, pre-departure de-briefing and post return de-briefing.

Briefing, for the purposes of this book, is the preparation of overseas workers to the level that they will flourish overseas and not merely survive. Briefings consist of both theoretical information (e.g. how cultures work in general), practical information (e.g. these vaccinations are required) and information about the specific locality (e.g. certain forms of clothing are expected). Briefing takes a minimum of two days through to a maximum of ten days, depending on the outreach location and duration and may be part of a longer course. People going overseas to work, particularly for the first time, function better if briefed for situations more challenging than those they are likely to experience. Participants learn the

BRIEFING AND DEBRIEFING – WHY NOW?

principles of how to function abroad as a Christian worker. Time is spent on difficult spiritual issues such as God's heart for the poor, prayer in the midst of suffering and the challenging issue of suffering itself. Practical guidance on staying healthy, team life, culture shock and returning home is given. Teams are taken through country specific briefings concerning customs, language and history as well as being oriented to YWAM as an organisation. Much non-specific learning occurs through living together in community, worshipping together and chatting informally to long term YWAM staff. Some language training may be involved although it is generally true that it is easier and quicker for adults to learn a new language *in situ* than in a classroom prior to arrival in the host culture.

Orientation on arrival takes a few hours through to a year if language learning is involved. Orientation will include more detailed information on the local culture, project, health care and security. A common challenge here is the tension between the arriving worker, sometimes with a headquarter's collusion, wanting to arrive as soon as possible and the receiving team's capacity to orientate the worker. As will be seen later 'first impressions count' and, if the team is unable to welcome the new worker adequately, then the new worker's time with the team may not be maximised.

Debriefing prior to departure home is mainly a technical, operational debriefing principally for the benefit of the local staff or partners. It will include a description of what was accomplished and some attempt to evaluate the work.

Debriefing on arrival home may well also include an operational debriefing and will also include more of a psychological and spiritual reflection on the worker's time away and their return to their home country. To that end the purpose of debriefing is to review the worker's time overseas opeationally, psychologically and spiritually such that they are able to bring closure to the experience and to move on to new things. The organisation or agency also has material available to it with which it can review the efficacy of its work and the efficacy of its selection and briefing procedures.

YWAM (UK) now offers three forms of debriefing. People on short term service programmes routinely attend a debriefing seminar within a month or so of returning home. The debriefing seminar has three aims: celebration and thanksgiving for the ministry that has been accomplished, team reunion and putting the experience overseas into context. This final aspect can be difficult. Those returning home can feel isolated, angry, guilty or numb. The isolation arises from not having people around who 'really' understand what they have been through. Guilt can develop from thoughts of leaving vulnerable people behind or from guilt at the comparatively easy and luxurious lifestyle we lead. Anger follows the re-encountering of the apparently shallow lifestyle of the West and the resultant feelings that people don't 'really' care. Some come to think that perhaps God doesn't care. A minority feel numb – they cannot take in either the experience overseas nor the contrasts on return. Most people attending the short term debriefing seminars are experiencing these feelings and find it helpful to relax with those who have been through similar experiences. Practical help and advice is given to help people re-orientate to being back home and some key ideas are given on how to settle back.

We also offer re-entry courses to those returning from long term service overseas. All the issues above apply but with more potency. Participants are helped to make sense of their time overseas as well as of a Britain which is quite different to the one they left up to ten years ago.

Finally a small number of people in YWAM and in other agencies become traumatised by things they have experienced. Agency staff worldwide work with horror, death, destruction, unremitting, unjust suffering and disease. Some staff themselves are attacked, taken hostage, robbed or traumatised in other ways. For some, despite selection and briefing, it is too much and they come home with deep hurts. We have been working quietly with such people for several years. The symptoms vary but the effect is the same – post traumatic shock. If proper help is given quickly then this chronic anxiety state can be healed. Even so, long term support is often needed. Deep questions of faith stop being academic – where is God when it hurts? Does God care, or even exist? Some staff need help to stop the nightmares, the flashbacks, the pain. Sometimes it is the home church which needs help. Pastors may feel out of their depth and families may feel unsure how to cope.

The UK government and the UK Evangelical Missionary Alliance have now adopted 'codes of best practice' relating to aid workers and to short term missionaries respectively[9][10]. The question for UK based organisations is no longer whether to provide routine psychological briefing and debriefing for their field workers but rather how. This book aims to provide some practical answers to that question and to provide some of the theoretical framework for what is termed 'best practice'. An account is given of the practical issues involved in selection and the psychological and spiritual briefing of people preparing for service abroad with missionary and aid agencies. The book's premise is that a satisfactory debriefing relies heavily on satisfactory selection and briefing procedures. An account is then given of routine debriefing procedures with particular reference to short term workers going for less than one year and for those returning after extended periods of service. The debriefing of workers who go abroad repeatedly is problematic and has not been dealt with here. An outline of the particular issues involved with the handling of those who become traumatised is also given followed by an outline theology of the key spiritual challenge that many workers face – that of suffering.

A high rate of people work on the field with such agencies only once and so the accounts are geared towards preparing the first time worker. A particular emphasis is placed on the preparation of teams although it is recognised that many field staff work singly.

1. As this book was going through its final draft the first reports of potential litigation against a small UK agency working in the Balkans began to be reported in the press.
2. Gal, R., and Mangelsdorff, A.D., *Handbook of Military Psychology*, Chichester, John Wiley, 1991.
3. O'Donnell, K., and O'Donnell, M., *Helping Missionaries Grow*, Pasadena, William Carey Library, 1988.
4. O'Donnell, K., *Missionary Care*, Pasadena, William Carey Library, 1992.
5. Foyle, M., *Honourably Wounded*, Eastbourne, MARC, 1990
6. Jordan, P., *re-entry*, Seattle, YWAM Publishing, 1992
7. Busuttil, W., *Intervention in PTSS, Implications for military and emergency service organisations*, 1995, Unpublished M. Phil Thesis, University of London.
8. Lovell, D.M., *Psychological adjustment amongst returned overseas aid workers*, Unpublished D. Clin. Psych. thesis, University of Wales, Bangor, 1997.
9. Davidson 1997 op cit.: see also appendices 6 and 7.
10. EMA/EA Code of Best Practice, 1997, op cit.

Chapter 2

Common challenges in the selection process

'The question is not whether you are called to go but whether you are called to stay' – Keith Green.

As [Jesus] walked along he saw Levi son of Alphaeus sitting at the tax collector's booth. "Follow me" Jesus told him and Levi got up and followed him.
Mark. 2:14.

With some trepidation I picked up the phone to make the transatlantic call. This was going to be difficult. The couple applying for missionary training were excellent but their young child was allergic to many things. From the medical examination it was clear that they could not go to the field as a family; the health risks to their son were too high. The wife answered the phone and the painful conversation ensued. At the end came her gracious but firm comment – 'we believe we have a call. Logically you are correct to turn us down but would you please pray again and see whether God would speak more clearly'. No pressure, no emotional outburst – just an invitation to rip up our entire application procedure and pray – yet again.

The selection team gathered for prayer. There was no angelic visitation, only a quiet peace to invite the family to proceed with their preparations to come over. The responsibility for the decision to come lay with the family. We prayed that the Lord would make it clear if He did not want the family to continue.

The second phone call was no less easy – we were not saying 'come'. We were asking the family of a six year old boy to continue testing their call. Only they, before God, could decide on behalf of their child. The parents were gracious again and accepted what we were saying. We wrote to confirm our telephone conversation and also contacted their minister.

On the transatlantic flight to the UK their son dramatically improved and remained well for several years afterwards. On one occasion as I watched their son play happily in Africa I pondered whether there was any point to application procedures.

Balancing that thought however was the experience that every single pastoral problem I have had to deal with always involves someone, somewhere, taking risks with procedures.

INTRODUCTION

Selection can be a contentious issue, particularly in Christian agencies who subscribe to an explicit charismatic theology. Several streams of thought exist. One stream is that of believing that a person's 'call' to a ministry is sufficient on its own to allow them to continue into that ministry. In practice people may then be accepted on the basis of their declared vision or 'calling' alone. Another stream is difficult to label but relies on 'divine circumstance' whereby a ministry simply emerges as people come together to fulfil a shared sense of calling. Both of these streams of thought are antagonistic to secular application procedures. They prefer to rely on 'Divine confirmation' rather than secular selection procedures. The underlying pre-supposition is that if God has called someone to do a task then others should not stand in the way.

Other streams of thought exist in missionary circles which place greater reliance on rigorous selection procedures. Usually these application procedures involve gathering an outline of many aspects of the candidate's biography, character and professional references together with a health check. Interviews may be considered but difficult to conduct if candidates are drawn from around the world making it unreasonable to expect candidates to travel large distances for such a process. The option of delegating interviews to centres local to the applicant's home is usually rejected since there can be no guarantee of consistency in such an approach.

The debate between these streams of thought can be a false one since it essentially approaches selection as either the responsibility of the candidate (I have a call, accept me) or the mission (we will decide whether you have a call). In turn candidates can end up making assumptions about the way the agency selects people. They can assume that confirmation of their 'call' is purely between them and God if application procedures are non-existent or thin. If extensive application procedures do exist they can tend to look like job applications which give the impression of a competitive process or a process involving some form of minimum requirement. 'God' does not appear to be an obvious part of the process.

To the author it would seem better to view the process of candidates coming into mission as a partnership between the Holy Spirit, the agency, the candidate, the sending church and the candidate's supporters. We are not looking to see whether the candidate is 'up to the job' but rather whether the body of Christ is in unity about the nature and timing of the candidate's call. With that in mind the debate then centres on how we can best utilise the secular theories on selection and couple them with a biblical understanding of 'call' or of the classical understanding of 'vocation' within the Church.

The literature on selection is vast and cannot be adequately represented here.[1] For our purposes I am assuming that candidates are being selected for foreign service or for training for foreign service.

A key issue to deal with is the large pool of potential applicants that agencies have access to. Aid agencies and, to an extent, missionary agencies are inundated with enquiries about service abroad. It is estimated that over 1,000 people per week approach aid agencies in the UK enquiring about the possibilities of service.[2] If an agency works in an area which grabs the media attention then 'deluged' would be a better word. At the height of the Romanian influx of aid workers YWAM (England) was fielding 40 unsolicited enquiries per day from potential field staff, most without previous foreign experience and many who were unqualified in any profession. We had half a dozen full time field vacancies in Romania and fewer than sixty short term vacancies. We also knew that other agencies were similarly unable to place further field workers.

By and large the majority of people approaching overseas agencies are good calibre and likely to do well. A few are there to escape the reality of home, some are pursuing a romantic fantasy. Both types are easy to spot. Much agency time is therefore taken up sorting outstanding candidates from the excellent and the excellent from the merely good. After a time one becomes blasé and can feel like rejecting people who do not have several degrees, relevant and extensive field experience, regular angelic visitations and a list of publications.

Agencies such as YWAM were formed, at least in part, as a reaction to such selection pressures. In the process, selection was largely abandoned in favour of inspiring people to go if they felt called. The result, some 35 years later, is 10,000 staff full time world wide and innumerable short termers each year. YWAM screens long term staff by putting them through an intensive 6 month induction programme. Short term volunteers are considerably less rigorously selected although most will encounter some form of screening process.

The general missionary community together with the secular agencies face a further challenge – not just how to fill a small number of vacancies from a large number of enquiries but also what to do with the large numbers left behind. After all, if we don't come up with some clear thinking on this, many will go out there on their own anyway. On rare occasions this goes very well; more usually, things go wrong.[3]

In summary, then, missionary agencies and aid agencies have a seemingly limitless pool of potential workers represented by enquiries from which to select future field workers. Many enquiries can be rejected out of hand. However selection processes are difficult to validate internally since so many of those who go on to apply appear to be good quality candidates who would probably do well almost irrespective of what selection procedures are used.

Given these caveats there are three principle selection methods available to selectors: application forms, interviews and games or simulations. None are foolproof and this is not the place to examine them in detail. Used well they do give agencies the information needed to make a reasonable judgement about applicants' competence for the situation being considered. Each method is examined briefly below, mainly from the perspective of problems which are still evident within the missionary and aid community.

APPLICATION FORMS

For a few hundred pounds an occupational psychologist or trained personnel manager can custom design an entirely adequate application form for an organisation. For a few hours work and the price of a photocopy or two any senior executive in an agency can design a poor application form which may give entirely the wrong impression of the agency and fail to distinguish good candidates from inadequate ones.

Poor forms can also lead to the candidates forming impressions of the agency which are entirely unintentional on the part of the agency. The agency simply wants information but does not necessarily think through how and when that information should be gathered. As a result candidates may conclude the following, perhaps wrongly:

The agency does not employ and promote women. (On the reference form to be given to the candidate's employer the candidate is referred to as 'he' or 'him'.)

The agency is racist. (The agency asks for a photograph as part of the application process – this can be taken as code for 'the wrong skin colour need not apply'.)

The agency has no eye for detail and is unprofessional. (The candidate is given a box sized 6 square centimetres for their initials and another the same size for their work history.[4])

The agency has taken care to ask the right questions for the job being applied for. (Or is the same application form sent to everyone from the Director to the cleaner?)

They appreciate that the applicant is a person. (One agency I know has its application pack sent parcel post – apparent code for 'join us and we will totally dominate your life'.)

The application pack is the first detailed impression candidates will get of an organisation. Clumsily designed forms with clumsy language will deter excellent applicants. Poor or desperate applicants may not notice or care. Designing application forms is best done with outside, professional help. The following are little more than tips to see how your current forms shape up.

LAYOUT

Often the last thing to be done is consideration of the layout and yet this is of crucial importance. There are plenty of software programmes around which will do a good job of designing the layout. The other bonus with these sorts of programmes is that forms can easily be adapted for particular types of application. From the candidate's perspective the most obvious and irritating flaw in forms is space being given for the answer which is disproportionate to the question. Selectors need to decide how much space is required for the answer and then either give that space or ask the candidate to answer on a separate piece of paper with a guide to what is expected. Increasingly candidates are asking for application forms by e-mail – this has got to be good news in terms of efficiency and speed but may mean that forms need to be redesigned.

QUESTIONS

In terms of the content there are a number of harsh questions to ask yourself. What, precisely, do you need the information for? Put another way, if you did not have the information would your decision be significantly affected? Much information is gathered about candidates which do not necessarily have a bearing on their ability to do a task successfully. This extraneous information gives a fuller picture of the candidate and is useful where the whole person of the candidate is being considered, for example in Christian agencies where there is an anticipated commitment to community. However there is a considerable danger that such information will become part of the wrong decision making process. Agencies I have consulted to have allowed the extra information to persuade them that the warm, friendly, mature person represented on the application form has the potential to do the job in hand. This is known, in psychological circles, as the 'Halo Effect' – the pleasantness of a personality overriding their competence. The selectors' task is to consider both the person's ability to fit in and also their ability to do the job. Different evidence is required for each component and some care needs to be taken to ensure that poor decisions are not taken on the basis of spurious evidence.

Consider the following typical and apparently innocuous offerings in the average application form for an international agency.

Marital status
Age
Gender
Nationality
Affix one passport size photograph here please.

Even these apparently neutral questions which are considered essential for many good and practical reasons may result in spurious information being returned which have the potential to bias the selector's decision with respect to the candidates' ability to do the task required.

Marital status – in what way does this piece of information help to appoint a cleaner, a clerk or a relief worker on permanent standby? Sometimes it does, sometimes it doesn't. In the first two cases it doesn't at all so agencies may be being nosy. In the third case it does but this is a senseless way of getting the information. What the agency may actually want to know in asking the question is whether the person has any responsibilities which affect their ability to fly off at a moments notice. So ask that. Other agencies may have a principled policy about divorcees. If that is the case then such principles should be made clear in advance so that 'unsuitable' candidates do not wade through an entire application process which they are ineligible for anyway.

Age. How does this, per se, affect the person's ability to work or study? Mainly it doesn't so don't ask it, it's irrelevant. There are valid reasons for asking, mainly to do with the costs of health insurance or, sometimes, team building. If that's the case then ask the question in a way which targets that purpose (e.g. 'Are you aged over 69?').

Gender. How does this, per se, affect the person's ability to work or study? Mainly it doesn't so don't ask, it's irrelevant. You may sometimes need to know gender if, for example, you are putting people into shared living accommodation and wish to separate the genders. Certain jobs may be restricted by gender (for example, the realities of work in Afghanistan under the Taliban). In these cases ask the question directly with an outline (perhaps as a footnote) of why you need to know.

Nationality. How does this, per se, affect the person's ability to work or study? Mainly it doesn't so don't ask, it's irrelevant. You may, on rare occasions, need to know because of visa restrictions in countries of operation. If that is the case say so and specify your current understanding of the relevant visa restrictions. 'Nationality' may, in any case, be a weak way of ascertaining possible visa restrictions since some applicants may be entitled to hold a number of passports. A helpful question for certain sorts of outreach might be 'Does your current passport have an Israeli Visa stamp in it?'.

It may be that some of the information above is needed in order to conduct a census of the profiles of candidates. If that is the case, conduct the census *after* the acceptance decision has been made or ensure that there is a mechanism to return census data separately to the application and to a separate part of the agency.

Finally – photographs. It is astounding how many agencies still ask for photos at the decision making stage when, usually, all they want is a photo for the student notice board or for staff to put names to faces. The danger of asking for photographs at this stage is that the photographs somehow become part of the decision making process either consciously or unconsciously. There is no demonstrable correlation between selector's assessment of candidates' competence or personality as judged by photographs and candidates' actual competence or personality.

And so the list of questions goes on. The questions following basic biographical information tend to focus on education, work experience and other background experience. Christian agencies will be particularly interested in the applicant's spirituality. In planning these types of question it is necessary to agree in advance the type of answers which are being looked for so that there is an objective criteria against which to judge the responses candidates give.

Technically, thinking in the above way can be described as 'anti-sexism', 'anti-racism', 'anti-ageism' and so on. Whilst true, it is also good-practice decision making. The decision makers are presented only with the information they require to make a decision. Irrelevant material is weeded out and there is less chance of decisions being made based on spurious information. It also has the advantage of being a transparent application process which will tend to build trust and partnership between agency and candidate from an early stage.

Personality check lists on reference forms

A recent phenomenon, particularly on reference forms, is the increasing use of adjective check lists. Typically the referee is asked to rate the candidate on a number of variables using a scale. Rarely is the adjective check list thought through with due regard to the quite complex psychology and mathematics involved nor with regard to the qualities required in successful applicants.

An example of a scale which has been thought through is shown in Table 2-1 (next page). (YWAM entry level course.) Scales need to be adjusted for the type of job being applied for. This is done by making a task analysis of the job to be done or by analysing the qualities required of a student on a particular course.

In the example in figure 2-1 assessors are asked to rate the candidate on a four point scale. The adjectives have been generated with respect to certain essential qualities that candidates for a YWAM introductory course require. Note that the adjectives are both positive and negative whilst the scale remains consistent. Thus assessors have to think actively about each item; they cannot simply enter the same number for each item. The scale is brief. A four or five item scale is best. Beyond that assessors are usually being asked to make too fine a judgement. By contrast, using a shorter scale (e.g. three items) can have detailed thinkers generating their own points.

The scale does not have absolutes at the poles (e.g. never, always) since it is unlikely that people are ever 'always' healthy etc. Using absolutes may mean that assessors will not use the poles and so end up effectively being restricted to a three point system anyway.

Examples of good items would be those where there is likely to be high agreement between referees (what is termed 'inter rater reliability') and where the item is measuring what it is intended to measure (what is termed 'validity'). My favourite examples of adjectives on a checklist which reflect poor inter-rater reliability and poor validity include:

> **Table 2-1**
> **Sample Personality Check List**
>
> Please assess the candidate on the qualities listed below according to the following evaluation system.
> 1 – usually 2 – often 3 – sometimes 4 – rarely
>
> Healthy____   Leader____   Reliable____   Loner____
>
> Team Worker____   Disruptive____   Initiator____   Aggressor____
>
> Enthusiastic____   Worrier____

Disposition (what ever does that mean? Poor inter rater reliability and poor validity)

Physical appearance (presumably pretty people are better than ugly people, or is it the other way round? Either way it predicts nothing about competence. Poor predictive validity)

Just to add to the confusion both the above are rated on a ten point scale.

Referees

A major challenge with referees is their tendency to be economical with the truth. Usually they are less than candid for benign reasons – they may wish the candidates happiness or success and so exaggerate the candidate's good points and minimise their bad points. Litigation fearful cultures may refuse to put anything bad about a candidate. Others may be reluctant to commit anything to paper which reflects harshly on the candidate out of loyalty or fear of being found out. Occasionally an employer may wish to rid themselves of a poor employee and so exaggerate the candidate's prowess. Invariably the tendency seems to be an exaggeration of the candidate's positive points.

Mitigating against this tendency is difficult. Three strategies help but are not foolproof.

The first is to send a brief covering letter with the reference form explaining what the candidate may be expected to encounter. The point of the letter is to recruit the referee's willingness to comment on the candidate's ability to function well in the appointment but not at the expense of their well-being.

Secondly a fairly stern warning can be put in the body of the reference form. One we use is:

'... conditions are primitive and often stressful, it is therefore not in the candidate's best interest to give an unrealistically positive view of them'.

Thirdly, offer a telephone conversation for those referees who would prefer not to commit themselves in writing. In general agencies need to be prepared to phone referees whenever they are unclear or uncertain about a reference. It is helpful to remember that agencies are in partnership with candidates and that, usually, all parties have the candidate's best interests at heart.

INTERVIEWING

Interviewing is both an art form and a scientific process. There is little doubt that interviewers improve with practice and gain wisdom in the process. Equally there is much empirical evidence concerning the reliability and validity of the interviewing process which cannot be gained simply through 'common-sense'.

Essentially there are five dynamics which competent interviewers need to be aware of.

1) The overwhelming variable to be compensated for in interviews is the extent to which the interviewer(s) like the candidate. From other parts of the literature in psychology we know that, essentially, liking people is a function of the extent to which they are similar to us. Undisciplined interviewers will therefore tend to pick people who are similar to them (i.e. 'likeable'), not necessarily candidates who are good at the job or have a training potential.

2) First impressions count. By and large interviewers will tend to come to a conclusion about a candidate within the first few moments of an interview commencing. This impression is difficult to shake, is largely unconscious and contributes significantly to the final decision of an interviewer.

The following three dynamics mitigate against the first two.

3) There should always be an interview panel (i.e. two or more interviewers). Where possible this should consist of peers but one person should

take responsibility for decision making. Peer membership is desirable to ensure that individuals on the panel are not 'outranked'.

4) The interview panel has a consistent membership for all candidates.

5) The interview panel should agree, in advance, objective selection and rejection criteria.

The value of interviews is enormous, particularly where it is important to get a feel of candidates' personalities and the likelihood that they will fit the organisation or team. In this respect 'liking' the candidate is actually a crucial aspect of the selection process. The problem is that liking candidates can easily become the sufficient reason for appointing them unless the safeguards outlined above are in place.

GAMES AND SIMULATIONS

Games and simulations as part of the selection process are useful but obviously require the candidate to attend in person. As mentioned elsewhere this can be problematic for international agencies making international appointments, for agencies recruiting from within a large country or in areas where travel is problematic.

In general the closer the situation for which a candidate is applying can be mimicked, the more predictive that situation is of the candidate's future behaviour. It is always worth remembering that past behaviour is a good predictor of future behaviour. For example, amongst missionary circles, it is taken as axiomatic that the best predictor of the quality of a candidate's field service is their service in their local church.

If games are the way forward then it is best to consult experts in how to set those games or simulations up. It also saves reinventing the wheel. A task analysis is necessary for each game and a suitable rating system needs to be established. Such consultations are not cheap and it is often more cost effective to get the information required from the candidate's history and references. Appendix 2 outlines the thinking behind a particular scenario.

MAKING THE APPLICATION PROCESS AS TRANSPARENT AS POSSIBLE

It is a good idea to make the acceptance criteria explicit in advance. Principally this helps the candidate to become a part of the decision making process and to strip away any unnecessary mystique about how the decisions are made. An example for an entry level course to YWAM is given in figure 2-2. By and large we have found this has cut down dramatically on spurious or poor applications and it is rare to turn down applicants for the course for reasons other than space. Furthermore, the applicants generally go on to do well on the course. In certain rare cases candidates leave prematurely. This is almost always settled amicably and it is clear to the candidate that they have misrepresented themselves in some way and need to take responsibility for that. In other words their presence on the course is a shared responsibility and their departure similarly needs to be a shared responsibility.

Table 2-2

Sample selection criteria sent to candidates for a YWAM relief and development training course as part of the application pack

- A clear call to serve for two or more years in Christian Relief and Development in the Developing World (not necessarily with YWAM)
- The unreserved backing of your church
- Sufficient health to work in pioneer situations abroad. (To that end should be able to walk up to six miles in a day, have no known serious or incapacitating illness, be clear of any significant health problems for a minimum of two years prior to the course commencing)
- Candidates will have a profession or apprenticed trade which will be of service in the developing world and will have worked in their trade or profession for a minimum of one year after qualifying
- Have no history of depression or anxiety in the previous two years; No history of eating disorders within previous five years and have no history of schizophrenia or other psychoses at all.

Although hard work, it is worth explaining items on the application process and making the information gathering process a two stage one. By and large we collect the following information only *after* a decision has been made to accept the candidate:

Drivers licence, photograph, next of kin details, nationality, including passport details.

FINALLY
The above is very hard work to achieve given the amount of detailed thinking that needs to be done. A motivating factor can be the hard work

and emotional energy involved in working to help someone who has no business being in a particular job or on a particular course because the selection process failed to weed them out. There is equal concern to see that the best possible people for the job or course are recruited and that they are not put off by sloppy practice.

[1] See particularly chapters by Foyle, Ferguson et al in O'Donnell and O'Donnell 1988, op cit and Schubert in O'Donnell 1992, op cit. New insights are represented in papers by Anyomi and by Dipple in Taylor, W.D. (Ed), *Too Valuable to Lose*, California, William Carey Library, 1997.

[2] International Health Exchange: Unpublished research reported at PIA workshop, London, 1996

[3] The classic example is the situation in Romania in the summer of 1991 where it is reported that the Romanian government temporarily suspended its attempts to count the number of aid agencies, let alone monitor or co-ordinate their activities. The total number of agencies exceeded 3,000 and the overwhelming majority had been formed in the previous 18 months, probably because their founders were unable to join or partner with established agencies. Few had the professionalism or expertise to co-operate with the entirely valid monitoring requirements of the Romanian health authorities, themselves under extreme pressure following the events of late 1989.

[4] Several years ago one agency kindly asked me for my opinion on their application forms. The questions were mostly fine but the layout was dreadful – typescript straight out of the 1970's and with poorly thought through spacing for the information required. They graciously accepted my suggestions but the clerks in the personnel bit of the agency didn't like change so things stayed the same. Unfortunately that extends to the, now, out of date telephone number at the top of the forms sent to referees. Were I a candidate for one of their programmes I'd form a different opinion of the agency than the one I know to be true.

Chapter 3

Briefing

> Teach me my God and King
> In all things thee to see
> And what I do in anything
> To do it as for thee.
> *George Herbert, The Elixir 1633.*

Wisdom is the principal thing; therefore get wisdom; and with all your getting, get understanding. Prov 4:7

> It had been a long day and I had a long drive home to come. I had spent six hours training missionaries on the theory and practice of briefing and debriefing. Much of the day had been spent on prevention – what people would need to know when they went to the field and what they would experience on return. Yet this gracious, elderly lady wished to speak to me.
>
> 'I worked for twenty years in Africa,' she said. 'For ten years after my return I thought I was going mad. Now this course has helped me to understand that I wasn't going mad – it was a normal reaction to coming back. Not only that, but I wish I had known all this prior to going in the first place, it would have saved me so much heartache. In six years of study we never covered any of this'.
>
> Her thanks were welcome, her pain evident.
>
> As a scientist I am trained to take little note of anecdotes such as the above – after all it is a pretentious little story suggesting that six hours of training in 1996 is somehow better than 6 years of training in the 1950's. So I ignore the fact that this scenario is repeated, word for word, every time I or my colleagues teach in local church settings or talk about our work in any depth to returned missionaries. We simply get on with the business of training the current generation. But there's a PhD in it for someone....

BACKGROUND ASPECTS OF PSYCHOLOGICAL AND SPIRITUAL BRIEFING

Ideally, briefing is primarily residential and compulsory for those going abroad to work. The residential component is more to do with team dynamic issues – some people cannot live/work in teams despite claims to the contrary and discover this whilst in the relatively benign setting of a training centre. Briefing may be of individuals or teams, but it is recommended that individual briefing should only be done in exceptional circumstances. Briefing will contain elements of theory (e.g. culture, team dynamics) and practics (this particular culture, this particular team). An operational briefing will also be given and this is not covered in this book.

The briefing style

Adults, including older adolescents, learn differently from children and so need to be educated quite differently. Adults attend briefings with a more or less extensive life experience. Many participants will already have some degree of cross-cultural experience and many will be professionally trained or have a high level of academic training. The briefing needs to maximise that experience and build on it by relating what they are learning to what they already know. The most constructive atmosphere for this dynamic is one where staff and participants are all are learners together.

Straightforward teaching from the front is both dull and unrewarding for the participants and a very ineffective way of getting information across. A certain proportion of such a teaching style is required but it should not form the totality of the learning experience. Adults should be involved in the learning process through discussions, role plays, seminars, brainstorming, drama, reflective exercises and simulations.

Location

There are many unresolved questions about where best to teach people about overseas service. For some it is best labelled briefing and done prior to departure, for others it is best labelled orientation and done on arrival. For yet others there is more of a distinction between briefing and orientation than simply location and both are needed. Other options include in service training or even training people during home leave.

To me none of the above options are mutually exclusive and there is comparative value in all of them. Part of the problem, as so often in situations of this type, is that the question of where to teach people about overseas service is too vague. For example an overview of culture, including adjustment is probably best done prior to departure. The basics of language learning is probably best done on arrival together with the nuts and bolts of how the project really works. Making sense of the experience and thinking about the future is probably best done on return.

A further consideration is the extent to which the course prior to departure is residential. There are significant advantages to residential courses, including fewer distractions, more control over the timetable and much more efficient use of time. People's attitudes can be observed and it is a chance to see how people really fit into a team setting rather than how they or their referees claim they do. In addition, teams, where applicable, have a chance to form in a benign setting without the sometimes intense pressures of field service. Such a course is also a good test of commitment.

Balanced against that is the upheaval of such a course just prior to departure. Attending a pre-departure briefing may effectively mean two moves rather than one. People are also taken away from their family and friends just at a time when they would like to see them the most.

The financial cost of such a course is also comparatively high. From an agency's point of view a residential course, particularly at a weekend requires more facilities and is harder on the trainers.

There is little research on the comparative effectiveness of these different forms of briefing. As a result decisions probably have to be made pragmatically with some clear thinking on the types of briefing that will best fit the audience and the project.

Duration

For most short term projects where people have only a limited amount of time available training over a weekend prior to departure coupled with a brief orientation on arrival is about as much time as can reasonably be given. For those going overseas for longer than a few months, particularly as part of a pre-formed team, a one week briefing course is more reasonable and is likely to be attended.

Anything beyond a year, certainly beyond two years, of potential field service can reasonably require an extensive training course. This can range from the compact courses offered by agencies such as YWAM and Operation Mobilisation which can be completed in a few months to more academic courses such as those offered by Bible colleges or postgraduate courses in relief or development offered by many universities. A recent phenomenon is the 'in house' training being offered by some of the 'new' churches in the UK, for example Ichthus.

Given the above YWAM (UK) has adopted the following principles regarding training of short term (i.e. less than one year) teams:

The first is that the briefing, field trip and debriefing (see next chapter) of a team is considered to be one complete element. That is, people participate in all or none of the short term team package.

Briefing and debriefing are residential and vary in length according to the duration of the outreach. For those going on a brief field trip lasting for two months or less the briefing course is held over a weekend as is the debriefing course. For those going overseas for about a year (usually gap year students) the briefing is for four to five days and the debriefing about three days. In both cases the briefing course takes place within the three weeks prior to departure and the debriefing course within a month of return.

Throughout YWAM (UK), without exception, all participants on those training courses which include a short overseas practicum, are briefed within a week of departure overseas and debriefed immediately on their return from the practicum.

A typical weekend schedule for briefing is shown in Table 3-1. The five day course would have a similar content but be spread out, allowing for more detail and time for discussion. An example is outlined in Table 3-2.

Table 3-1
Sample weekend schedule for briefing summer outreach teams

Friday evening

Arrive, welcome, introductions, split into teams to meet one another

Saturday

Worship
Overview of the agency
Overview of how cultures work
Overview of how teams work
Team meetings (project, cultural specifics)
Simulator (see below)
Overview of missions
Health briefing

Sunday

Worship
Teaching on intercession
Team meetings to discuss pre departure planning

Table 3-2
A sample briefing programme for year long teams

Tuesday

11.30	Arrival and registration
12.30	Lunch
2.00	Orientation to teaching centre and locality
6.00	Dinner
7.30	Worship

Wednesday

9.00	Devotional, prayers etc.
10.00	Team relationships
12.30	Lunch
2.30	Aims and objectives of the teams
4.00	Meet in teams
6.00	Dinner
7.30	Video (with some relevance to mission or field work)

Thursday

9.00	Devotional, worship
10.00	Cultural adjustment
12.30	Lunch
2.00	Simulator
3.30	Tea
4.00	Health on the field
6.00	Dinner and free evening

Friday

9.00	Devotional
9.20	Keeping spiritually fit
10.20	Prayer and commissioning of teams
11.30	Team meetings
12.30	Lunch
2.00	Parents/relatives/friends presentation
4.00	Tea and depart

The incidentals

Two groups of staff are involved in the briefing. The first may have little to do in the way of teaching but rather is there to interact with the students and provide continuity. The second group may be visiting speakers who would also make themselves informally available to the participants.

Several factors guide the ordering of events. In both briefings the early emphasis is not centred around giving information even though participants come eager to 'be briefed'. Rather the emphasis is on getting to know the participants and the participants getting to know each other. Having become reasonably comfortable in each other's presence the next focus is on worshipping God and coming together in fellowship. Only after this do people begin their formal briefing. Even here the emphasis is on people relating to each other and to their host cultures. A common phrase used is 'ministry flows from a praying, worshipping community, not the other way around'. As the participants begin to touch the idea that they are going to reflect Christ rather than 'do task X', then the staff feel able to give concrete details about the tasks involved. To do things the other way around would be to build relationships and worship around the job, rather than building relationships and a sense of worship because of their inherent worth and reflection of Christ. Emphasis throughout is put on prayer and worship with these time tabled for the beginning, i.e. quality times, of each day. The expectation throughout is that first and foremost God is to be praised and glorified and that our lives flow from that expectation.

Sufficient time is set aside for the team members to get beyond the basics by the end of their time together. Typically each team member would have opportunity to talk a little about their life history, how they became a Christian, how they came to be of the team, their interests and their hopes and fears for the time ahead.

SIX COMPONENTS OF BRIEFING:

The following is an outline of what are seen by me as the essential components for briefing people for their overseas experience. There is no claim that the following is sufficient. I am reasonably confident, however, that it contains the necessary components to ensure the mental, physical and spiritual well being of overseas workers as a minimum and that it also gives workers effective tools for operating cross culturally at a personal level. Beyond that it is for individual agencies to ensure that workers have the basic competencies in the development approach to be used, appropriate security briefings and any other training, especially theological, language and specific cultural training, that may be needed.

There are six different aspects to the curriculum: cultural orientation; cultural adjustment; team dynamics; spiritual preparation; physical health and security; the aims and objectives of the team.

1) CULTURAL ORIENTATION

The training outlined below is not culture specific but rather gives workers a broad understanding of one approach to how cultures work in general. From that it is possible for workers to generate their own solutions. Nevertheless agencies may wish to top up the training with specific cultural guidelines – e.g. dress code, greeting styles. In principle these should not be taught by rote as it dis-empowers the workers and can produce caricatures of local sensibilities. So, for example, rather than suggesting that men do not wear shorts in rural east Africa, informing them that shorts are what little boys tend to wear allows them to draw their own conclusions about dress code.

The training emphasises throughout that it is fine to make mistakes. The cultures that participants are encountering are well used to 'stupid foreigners' in much the same way that we are. Mistakes are tolerated provided they are learned from, are not made maliciously and that the aftermath is handled with the appropriate sensitivity. Quite different training is required for people intending to work with cultures who have not previously been contacted.

A. *The underlying structures of cultures*

A basic premise under girding this aspect of the curriculum is that cultures differ in God-given ways and also reflect something of God's creative

'Onion Rings' Model of Culture, Kwast 1994

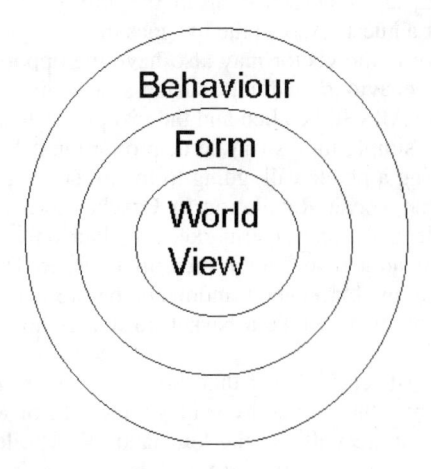

Figure 3-1

nature. As such, all cultures are precious and to be valued. No one culture has all the answers and therefore other cultural norms are to be honoured and valued in principal. Therefore, the aim is an introduction to some models of how cultures work, orientation to so-called culture shock and the stresses involved in re-entry, training in how to work effectively in a cross cultural setting and to help them develop their own personal coping mechanisms for living in a different culture.

The most straightforward anthropological model to teach that is currently available seems to be a twinning of the 'onion rings' model outlined by Kwast[2] (Figure 3-1) and work done by Lingenfelter and Meyers[3] on cultural values.[4] Burnett[5] has written helpfully about specific cultural variations but specific cultures are not covered in this particular curriculum.

Let us consider and develop the outline by Kwast first of all. On arrival in the host culture what is experienced first is the outward behaviour of the local people. Obvious will be the way people dress, whether the genders dress differently, the kind of language spoken, who speaks to whom. It will quickly become apparent how to eat and the rituals that accompany eating. Are utensils used? How does one ask for 'more' or 'some of'. Are hands used; if so, which one? Where do people sit: on chairs, on the floor, kneeling, sitting, reclining? Do the genders sit together or apart? Is there a place of honour; if so, who sits there – the distinguished guest or the head of the household? When full does one give an empty plate to the host to signal one is 'full' or rather ensure that a small amount of food is left to indicate that the host has provided 'more than enough'. Does one help with the washing up or does that insult the ability of the host to make arrangements for a guest? And so the list goes on.

After some while the visitor may also have the opportunity to observe more complex behaviour – doing business, teaching, voting, making friends and so on. All will be alien and the visitor can feel quite powerless and stupid. Even simple things can be disproportionately difficult – posting a letter, making a phone call, going to the toilet, shopping. During the final stages of the Velvet Revolution in Czechoslovakia my wife and I were shopping in a Prague supermarket. We had only nipped in to get some milk and bread and so did not pick up a basket. The manageress of the shop berated us for several moments before we understood that customers were obliged to take a basket no matter how few items were being purchased.

After a while it becomes clear that the behaviour in the society is not random or odd but rather driven by values – the idea of what is 'good' or 'best'. A desert culture will use the left hand when toilleting or dealing with anything judged insanitary and the right hand for eating or anything judged clean. In those circumstances 'it is best' to have a convention about which hand to use in which circumstances. In many cultures there are clear values about the wearing of clothes. Women may be expected to cover different parts of their bodies to reflect modesty. For some this will involve covering their shoulders, for others covering their elbows, for still others covering the entire length of their arm. The rationale is not always clear. There is the well known story of the Victorian missionaries who insisted the women converts in the tribe they were working with covered their breasts. 'Why', asked the Chief after a while, 'does your God want our women to be prostitutes'? After some discussion it transpired that women's breasts, when covered, were a sign of a prostitute.

Sometimes cultural behaviour is simply driven by inertia although there are good historic values for the practice. Thus in the UK people drive on the left and have done so since the invention of the car. The practice is simple to account for historically – when riding horses, people would pass to the left of an oncoming horse to keep their sword arm free. When cars appeared on the scene habit took over and the practice continued. Nowadays car drivers pass to the left of an oncoming vehicle because it is too difficult and expensive to change the practice. There may also be a slight Island mentality involved of hoping that the rest of the world will eventually see sense and come round to our way of thinking!

Underpinning the values of culture is the next layer of Figure 3-1 – beliefs or the answer to the question 'what is true'? This can be thought of as the culture's agreed way of perceiving the world.

At the core of any culture is its world view. World view deals with the answer to the questions of reality. It has been defined as our pre-suppositional beliefs, that is what we know to be true, simply because it is true. There are various ways of thinking about world view but it is often best evidenced by the culture's myths and religion. The myths and religion do not necessarily predict values and beliefs but they may indicate why beliefs and values are held. Generally such truths are communicated 'from the cradle' onwards by authority figures such as parents and teachers or by other role models.

A clear example of an historic change in world view is taxation policy in the UK. Nowadays UK taxes are designed to redistribute the wealth of the nation to either the State or to those deemed in need, for example the sick, the poor, the unemployed etc. Taxes are also altered in an effort to control the inflationary pressures within an economy. In essence money is taken from the rich and given to the poor for the benefit of society as a whole.

A well loved myth in the UK is that of Robin Hood. Tales are told of this man taking money from the very rich and giving it to the oppressed poor. Generally the tale is told with Robin Hood as a hero, a good man and one whose policy is to be applauded. Clearly there is something in this folk hero which modern British people collectively and almost 'instinctively' approve of. That same 'something' underpins British peoples' general acceptance of money being taken from rich people and given to poor people as part of taxation policy. That 'something', which is difficult to articulate, (i.e. is pre-suppositional) is an example of an element of society's collective world view.

By contrast, in the UK during Victorian times, the saying 'the rich man in his castle, the poor man at his gate' had widespread unconscious acceptance which was at variance with the prevailing world view of today. The poor were poor, the rich were rich and that was the status quo. Taxes were raised in order to support the functions of the state (war and the monarchy principally) and certainly not to redistribute wealth away from the rich. The myth of Robin Hood survived as a 'folk tale' told by the poor living in hope of another Robin Hood. It is only more recently that the folk tale has gained acceptance more widely.

Western missionaries and aid workers have long held the world view that the 'rich' helping the 'poor' is a good thing, intrinsically. It is a belief in a particular truth driven by a particular world view. It is clear that this is not a universally held belief at all times and in all cultures. It is also becoming clear in recent decades that such an approach, applied simplistically, fails in the long run.

It is also apparent that societies driven by world views such as Hinduism, Christianity, Islam, Confucianism, Marxism and secular humanism will have radically different practices relating to taxation, charity, abortion, the roles of men and women in society, and so on.

The message that those going abroad need to absorb is that 'foreigners' do things differently and do so purposefully. The reasons are sometimes conscious, sometimes unconscious, and always, to that culture, valid. Yet, to assume that one's world view is correct is a powerful, sometimes overwhelming dynamic. To have it challenged is to have our very being challenged and the trap that missionaries and aid workers have tended to fall into historically is to assume the absolute rightness of their personal world view and to seek to impose that on other cultures.[6] [7]

B. Encountering cross cultural values.
It is possible from this model to understand the dynamics underlying cross cultural encounters. In figure 3-2 we can see the two cultures moving towards one another. The first thing they encounter is each others' behaviour which, to the other, is more or less bizarre. After a while some understanding of the culture's values and beliefs becomes evident and that sheds light on the behaviour. The values and beliefs may well be mysterious and it becomes apparent that one cannot truly get to grips with the culture until the culture's world view has been incorporated into us. As an adult learner that may well be almost impossible.

The strategy used in training is therefore to expose trainees to the idea that cultures vary dramatically and do so in an ordered way. Their task on entry is to accept the differences and then try to understand them, in particular to try and understand the underlying values of a culture which give rise to particular behaviours.

'Onion Rings' Model of Culture Encounter, Kwast 1994

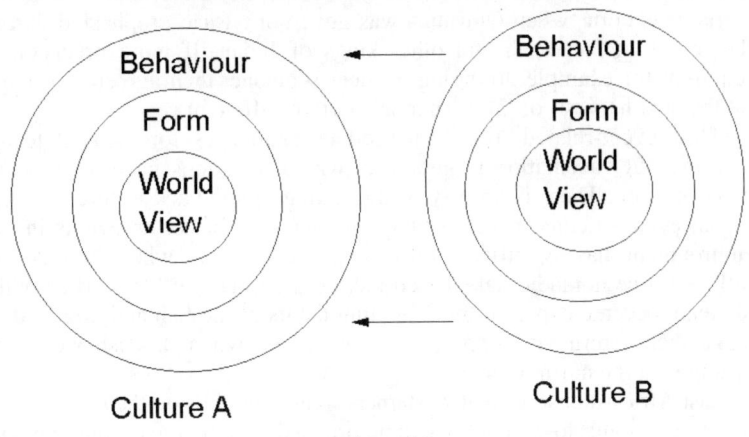

Culture A — Behaviour / Form / World View

Culture B — Behaviour / Form / World View

Figure 3-2

Further help is given by outlining the dynamics written about by Lingenfelter and Meyers which seem to outline some of the classic differences in values, beliefs and, to an extent, world view. Six dynamics are outlined in a study of South Pacific islanders which seem to have applications across many cultures. The author has added a seventh suggestion following experiences in Eastern Europe immediately after the collapse of communism.

The seven dynamics represent the tensions involved in differing perceptions of time, relationships, vulnerability, decision making, task orientation, status and pragmatism. In addition a section is added concerning country specific issues and common errors made by Westerners encountering a new culture.

(i) Time

There are a variety of different ways of looking at time. For some cultures time moves along in a forward linear fashion. For other cultures time is circular: the same things come round every year and nothing much changes or, in another version, time moves on but things in the universe keep returning to the same place to live and relive their lives. Many religions have some notion of eternity, a non linear time where things continue without end. In Islam and some branches of Christianity there is the notion of a future which is fixed and about which little can be done. In many aspects of Hinduism and other branches of Christianity the future is not at all fixed but behaviour does have consequences.

Other, mainly rural, cultures have little use for the notion of linear time and have a notion of time centred on events. The whole of the Christian Old Testament and the Gospel accounts are written using this measure of time. Here things happen in relation to events, not a calendar or a clock. Christ was born 'when Quirinius was governor'. Isaac prophesied during the reigns of Hezekiah and other kings of Judah. If more precision is required, for example arranging to meet someone, then agreeing to meet 'at the next harvest' or 'after sunrise' is often sufficient.

This 'event-related' time can produce challenges for medical teams carrying out vaccination programmes where injections have to be staggered in time. There is no way of translating 'come back in three weeks' for an event oriented tribe. Finding another way, based on events in the environment, has to suffice – for example 'come back when the moon is full'. For one nomadic, lake-based fishing tribe that YWAM worked with, the team became expert at the migrating habits of the fish and arranged to make their return visit appointments based on when the fish were, for example, at the north of the lake.

East Africans observe that westerners wear their gods on their wrists. For westerners going to a non-linear time-oriented society, organising appointments and schedules can be trying. It is obvious to the locals when a meeting starts – it starts when everyone is present. It is obvious when the bus will arrive – when it gets there. It is obvious (for Christian workers) how long to preach for – for as long as God wills. To quote another East African saying about Westerners – 'You have the watches – we have the time'.

To go to an Islamic society can be equally trying for both sides. The meeting will start when God ordains it. There comes a slight whiff of blasphemy from the proceedings if the westerner tries to hurry things along or force decisions – who are they to hurry the will of Allah?

One African Bishop put the whole thing in context for me once when I innocently asked what time he thought the bus I was about to board might get to its destination. 'I don't know' he said. 'Just remember that the purpose of this bus is to get you to Dar es Salaam. If it breaks down along the way they'll fix it or get another one. In the meantime, get out your picnic and make some friends'. I naively pressed the point, raising the issue of my connecting flight back to England. 'Well, if you miss it there's another one isn't there?' was the friendly rejoinder.

(ii) Relationships

Interacting strongly with the first dynamic is that of the primacy of people or of projects. Are people more important than the enterprise they are engaged in or is it the other way round? Generally in the West 'time is money' and therefore projects have to move 'efficiently'. Thus the needs of people have to be subsumed to the needs of the project.

In the west meetings start 'on time' and immediately move to the business at hand. There is rarely any time given to people introducing themselves or getting to know one another. The agenda is everything. Contrast this with doing business outside the Christian West. How is it possible to do business with someone who is unknown? What family do they come from? Where do they come from? What is their background? Only when the person is known can the business begin.

A similar phenomenon exists with buying items. In the West people have diminished in importance to such a level that it is actually possible to shop in a supermarket without speaking to a soul, including the cashier. Try it one day! Shortly, if the technophiles have their way, we won't even have to leave home, we'll do our shopping by computer and not have to speak to a soul, ever.

Contrast this with buying an item in a market elsewhere on the planet. One is not buying just any old watermelon or any old piece of lace. 'This watermelon or lace is a labour of love. And for you, sir or madam, as I get to know you so I will feel more inclined to talk to you about its price. We shall drink tea and talk about life. Then you can have the item when we understand its value to one another'. Along the way, relationships are built and the watermelon or lace has a story to it.

On arrival in a different culture the project-oriented, time-oriented westerner becomes disoriented by the apparent inefficiency, even laziness, of the host culture. The host culture is disoriented by the aggression and rudeness of the visitor who seems only interested in things and not at all in people.

(iii) Vulnerability

Cultures vary according to whether they see admission of errors as a character strength or a character weakness. Broadly 'confession is good for the soul' according to the Christian West yet, for many cultures, admitting failure is a grave loss of face leading to humiliation not just for one's self but also for one's family. 'Saving face' becomes a prime motivation overriding issues such as truth or fault attribution. By contrast British Anglo Saxons have a tendency for understatement or gentle self caricature suggesting that weakness is seen as a sign of strength.

Making the assumption that cultures are the same as one another in this area can lead to difficulties, particularly when establishing relationships. On one occasion I was involved in the early stages of negotiations with a senior government official in Eastern Europe and working through a highly competent interpreter. I knew enough of the local language to be able to track the conversation. On the spur of the moment it occurred to me that it might be a good idea to endear myself to the official by telling him a story of one of YWAM's errors and the lessons that had been drawn from that. I launched into the story and listened in amazement as the interpreter, after the first few sentences, began to make up a story of his own. I was baffled but trusted the interpreter enough simply to continue with the charade assuming that the story was either difficult to translate or was somehow culturally inappropriate.

In a suitable gap I asked the interpreter about the apparent mis-translation. 'Never pull such a trick again in my country', he said. 'You have to remember that not so long ago people were put in prison or shot for making mistakes. None of my countrymen would ever admit to an error, to do so would be either an indication of stupidity or, worse, an automatic assumption of the need to be punished. If you must tell stories then tell of your successes, you won't be considered big headed'.

The culture clash between the USA and Iraq at the end of the Gulf War was fascinating from this perspective. The USA wanted Iraq to apologise. For that to happen Iraq would have lost face. There was never any way that an apology would be forthcoming and the bewilderment of the US government was very apparent.

(iv) Decision making

The West idolises the cult of the individual. The media is full of tales of individual heroism or self-made individuals. Sports are arranged competitively in leagues with prizes going to those who beat others. Decisions are made individually and important decisions, such as voting, are made individually and in secret. If someone wishes to vote in a particular way, have an abortion or follow a particular religion then it is culturally appropriate to believe that the decision is 'up to them', or that 'it's their decision'. The best sleeping accommodation is private – an individual bedroom for each individual or couple.

This is to be contrasted with cultures where the emphasis is more on the group. Individuals should not stand out from each other. Sport is not so competitive since individuals should not stand out. Decisions are far too important to be left to an individual. Families are consulted, respected elders give their input. Individuals do not 'come to Christ' but families or entire communities do. Sleeping is a communal activity. Putting someone in their own room is highly disrespectful suggesting that they are unpopular or not worthy of sharing with others. Voting, where that is acceptable, is a public affair. Often there is a distinct preference for unity in decision making and so, where voting does occur, a simple majority will not do. The majority would have to be overwhelming.

The West is used to mocking regimes where some 90% of the votes cast are for the new president or head of state. Yet to many cultures, where group consensus is critical, any other result may be senseless. If such cultures wished they could equally well mock the democracies of the west where, when individuals can be bothered to vote, governments can be returned on a minority of the votes cast.

For Westerners going to such cultures life can be frustrating. It is difficult to find people to take responsibility for decisions or, even, to make decisions. Westerners who enjoy solitude may find the constant need of the local people to provide companionship and hospitality overwhelming after a while. The value of including everyone in decisions at the expense of 'efficiency' can be frustrating. Yet, the locals are not setting out to be frustrating – they are simply working things out through their own values. To try to understand things using 'western' values is to misunderstand the cultures we are seeking to serve.

(v) Status

Cultures take a different view on whether those in positions of responsibility should be there by virtue of their ability or their heritage. For the west the idea of someone near the bottom of society making it to the top is to be applauded. There is nothing farcical about having a grocer's daughter or a trapeze artist's son as British Prime Minister. This is to be seen as a mark of greatness – despite the odds, they made it to the top.

For other cultures such an idea is, at best, bizarre. At worst it is an inversion of the natural order of things. Leaders are born and bred, not made. Heritage is of crucial importance. After all how else can we know the person is 'made of the right stuff' or has had the right up-bringing? It is only comparatively recently that the caste system has been seriously challenged in India. Prior to that, and possibly still in some remote areas, it was quite impossible to achieve greatness except within the confines of a caste.

Operating in the latter form of culture means that discussions on family and national background become crucial. Personal testimonies to the effect of being lifted from the gutter will baffle some audiences rather than inspire them. Being unmarried can automatically debar even the most competent nurse from participating in family planning clinics. Being a particular nationality may be critical in determining whether you, personally, can be trusted or not.

The purpose, then, of 'relationship building' in many cultures goes well beyond making friends so that things go smoothly. Much of the activity centres around the host culture trying to understand what makes the visitor worthy of the position they hold. Merit is not enough and may even be irrelevant. Birthright and background can be of more consequence. In many societies gender may be of critical importance.

(vi) Pragmatism

During the early 1990s in eastern Europe I noticed an apparent difference in thinking patterns between west Europeans and east Europeans. Broadly, Westerners are taught to think in non absolute terms or 'pragmatically'. This relativistic thinking means that decisions are taken on the basis of the available evidence or on the basis of what is realistic or convenient. By contrast east Europeans were taught to think more in terms of absolutes or principles. Things were right or wrong according to set ideas, not according to circumstances.

The differences often showed through in negotiations. The author or team would go for a convenient solution to a problem especially if apparently trivial. The eastern colleagues would go for a principled decision. One debate that frustrated both sides, particularly in the early days, was hospitality. The host culture prized hospitality and had been unable to practise this with foreigners until after their Revolution. For aid workers to arrive was a heaven sent opportunity for honouring foreign visitors. Their thinking was therefore to honour the visiting teams at every available mealtime. Lunch therefore could take up to three hours. By the team's standards of convenience and pragmatism, however, to have three hours out during every working day was senseless. Logistically it was better to party in the evening and work through the day. Eventually a combination of priority of people over project coupled with the host's cultural insistence on the principal of hospitality at every available opportunity won and the team pragmatically became used to a five hour day working on tasks and a much longer time 'working' on relationships.

(vii) Country specific issues
Participants need briefing about country specific issues. Usually these need to be given under at least the headings of dress code, food, alcohol, relationships (gender related, age related) and religious issues. At this point it is easy for two errors to be made. The first is discussing the 'minimum the team can get away with', the second is generating long lists of do's and don'ts which are overwhelming.

Cultural briefing is not to encourage retention of as much of one's home culture as possible but rather to encourage participants to integrate as fully as possible with the host culture in the time available. The question is not 'what can I get away with?' but rather 'how can I best bless and honour the host culture in the way I integrate?'.

Generating long lists of rules is invariably unhelpful. It seems better to sensitise participants to how different cultures work and then let them begin to work the rules out for themselves. Some straight instructions are needed where either the rules are not at all obvious (e.g. not pointing the soles of one's feet at another in South East Asia) or where the social consequences of breaking a rule can be severe (e.g. Christians drinking alcohol in Africa).

(vii) Common errors made by Westerners encountering a new culture
All short term teams going abroad are taken through a brief list of areas where teams can be caught out quite unwittingly.

Airport and in-country conversation is a frequent cause of unintentional difficulty. Participants are reminded that when in a check-in queue at the departure airport they are likely to be surrounded by nationals of the country where they are going to work. Almost certainly these nationals speak the language of the aid workers or at least understand it. Conversations describing the primitive, backward, awkward or oppressed country being visited insult the nationals in the queue. Worse, the aid worker or missionary agency is often readily identifiable (luggage labels, clothing with agency logos and so on) and thus the agency as a whole becomes tainted by the insults, not just the individuals. Nationals in the queue are unlikely to be swooning with gratitude but rather understanding what these foreigners 'really' think of the country.

The conversation on the way out back can be worse. I have stood in many a check-in queue in a foreign airport listening to aid workers thanking some deity at random that they are able, at last, to leave this particular hell hole and get back to 'civilisation'.

My most poignant afternoon in an airport was at the height of the baby exporting boom from Romania in the early 1990's. Rather than send money in to Romania to help fund a national adoption process, foreigners were taking Romanian children abroad by the hundreds every week.[8] The airport was awash with crying babies and weary adoptive parents who had nothing but horror stories to tell one another. The stories continued on the tarmac and into the aircraft. I sat frozen in my seat as I watched the faces of the TAROM stewardesses. Their thoughts were inscrutable as they attended to over 50 children aged under a year. Their faces, however, belied the pain of their country. There was no rejoicing at 50 'saved' children only horror that these children were leaving the country and that it was blindingly obvious to them just what the parents thought of Romania.

Diplomats and other government officials may also be present on the flights and love to fall into conversation with aid workers and missionaries who are usually a veritable mine of 'soft' but useful information. I remember chatting in an aeroplane for several hours to a pleasant man about local reaction to a counter coup attempt in a country I had just visited. The reaction of the military and the police had been quite intriguing and I was naively happy to off load my observations to anyone who would listen. Discovering that the pleasant man was also a NATO military attaché caused an abrupt change of subject.

People often ask when their outreach or tour of duty starts and ends. For YWAM(UK) teams it is from the moment they enter their departure airport to the moment they leave that airport. It is the period of time when, as another generation used to suggest, 'if you have nothing good to say, say nothing'.

Cameras are fascinating because of the way in which they are used. Very often photographs can be taken to indicate how brave, noble, difficult or harrowing the owner's activities have been. A few sunsets and some party pictures complete the portfolio. Why are those pictures taken? Imagine going into someone's home and immediately setting about photographing the dirty toilet, the cobwebs on the ceiling, the dirty washing. Imagine then having those photographs shown to public meetings around the locality with an impassioned plea for help. Such a thing would never happen and yet we do the same kind of thing to people of other, remote nations.

When briefing overseas teams I suggest that participants do one of two things with their camera:

Leave it behind (no one ever has)

Take it but take photographs out of relationship. They should not photograph 'a beggar' or 'a leper' or 'a patient' but rather photograph Raoul or Hose or Francesca; people they have got to know a bit and whose story they can tell. If photographs of the ugly in a country must be taken then equal care should be taken to photograph the good.

The vast comparative wealth of a missionary can easily become an issue. We forget just how wealthy we are in many of the countries we go to. The result can be unintentional pain for the host culture. Imagine working in an area of absolute poverty. We invite some local people for a soda. Without thinking we cause pain. The hospitality is welcome yet, for the price of a drink, the person could have bought some needed soap or toothpaste, sent a letter or bought some shoelaces.

We can also forget, in our flippant generosity, the dignity that the poor have and their desire to extend generosity to us. A small group was once taken to lunch by their national host. The hotel restaurant was expensive by local standards but the exchange rate meant that the total price of the meal was £10. At the end the team leader expansively suggested paying for the meal and 'won'. He glanced across to his host too late. Her woebegone expression said it all, she had carefully saved to treat them and had been robbed of that opportunity and consequent joy.

I have a friend who had better remain anonymous. This African born missionary, for whom the word 'gentleman' was invented, has sworn that he will meet the next plane load of ex-pats hoping to work with him with some plastic bags. Into those bags will go his little list of items which he knows will offend members of his conservative culture:

Sony walkmen,
jeans for the women
chewing gum
sunglasses
electrical equipment (he has told team leaders countless times there is no electricity)
more than one change of clothing except Sunday best
more than one bag per team member.

As my friend points out, it is not the visiting team which experiences the outrage of the locals; people in his culture are far too polite for that. It is him as the local leader who has to put up with the constant complaining about insensitive, rich, know-it-all foreigners.

Entire books can be written about the issues of clothing and alcohol. The rule is simple. If the local leaders within the agency say dress modestly then do so. If they say don't drink alcohol then don't – from the time teams arrive at the departure airport to the time they return from the field.

Obviously such a list can extend indefinitely. The above is a reflection of the most common errors that teams seem to encounter which do not readily fall into the models of culture outlined at the beginning of the chapter. Alerting the visiting teams to these issues has significantly reduced the difficulties teams have experienced and also improved their relationships with the local people.

2) CROSS CULTURAL ADJUSTMENT
A. Entry adjustment

Historically cross cultural adjustment has been thought of as 'culture shock' or entry shock.[9] However the implication behind the titles is that of a transient anxiety state which may be more or less severe. Marjory Foyle[10] has suggested that in fact the principal dynamic is one of mourning the life left behind. Newly arrived workers are less concerned about the pit latrine in front of them and are more consumed with the 'nice' flush toilet they have given up. Talk around the meal table, in an undisciplined team, is less to do with the sorghum which has been served up yet again, more with the foregone delights of home cooking or 'take aways'.

The adjustment reaction is therefore similar to a mourning process; mourning what has been left behind with the present a constant reminder of what has been given up.

The natural history of entry to a new culture may be thought of as three phases: honeymoon, adjustment and resolution. This is not a universal pattern – we once received a postcard in our office from a recently arrived team member with the one line 'when does the honeymoon phase begin'? written on it!

The honeymoon phase in cultural adaptation is probably inaccurately named though for different reasons to the corresponding team adaptation outlined below. The dynamic is less to do with unadulterated joy, although that may be the case, and more to do with the idealised way the culture and mission is often viewed. Coupled with that is the overwhelming assault on all five senses. Everything, but everything, is different and newly arrived workers are put into a state of high arousal where their senses become hyper alert.

Even the simplest task is a challenge. One negotiates prices rather than paying the advertised price. Buying a bus ticket may involve several different queues. Health-care and other professional occupations are conducted quite differently. Yet, at this stage, all is an adventure. Newsletters are written outlining the alienness of the culture and how exciting it all is. New friends are made, often very quickly. Depending on the nature of the work it is possible to move in quite different circles to those at home. Where it was once a challenge to get time with the vicar, one can now routinely meet the bishop. Meetings with senior officials of government agencies and ministries may become normal, indeed expected. If the ex-pat community is very small then the inevitable invitation to cocktails with the participant's national ambassador may arrive.

All this can happen at breathtaking speed. On my tenth day in one African nation I went from chatting to the US ambassador to being mistakenly arrested by the army, to being rescued by local airline officials and diplomats all within the space of five minutes.

Life at this level of intensity cannot continue. Eventually the excitement begins to pall. At this stage the grieving process seems to begin. There is sometimes an irrational anger that the locals cannot do things 'properly'.

Frustrating thoughts come:

'I don't want to spend all day in the market getting my groceries – back home I can do all this in 30 minutes'.

'Why can't the locals just cut to the core of what they mean – why do we have to spend time hearing about their cousins and sons and daughters'?

'I'm fed up with paw paw and beans and rice, I want a Big Mac'.

Conversations with the local people, even with the ex-pat community if foreign, start to become wearing. Whole swathes of communication become impossible. The local sports are different. One can't joke about the president. The English gift of understatement begins to grate as does the American gift of enthusiasm and so on. Participants just want to kick back, put their feet up and chat about nothing without having to continually explain themselves to the detriment of the conversation. Home is a long way away.

The tendency is to withdraw, to talk incessantly about 'back home', to become angry at the 'wrong way' of doing things locally and even to begin wishing one was at home. This adjustment process can begin at any time but usually occurs within the first few months of arrival. Its duration is similarly uncertain but is unlikely to last more than a few months. During this time the bereavement reaction can be intense and the team member may well be irritable and reluctant to engage the local culture. It is this particularly noticeable feature which has probably led to the term 'culture shock' rather than some term suggesting sadness at not being at home. The acid test is to look less at the behaviour of people going through the reaction and more at their pre-occupations. By and large they will be thinking, more or less longingly, for home. This will be heightened by particular personal events during the year such as birthdays, anniversaries and national public holidays. For Brits, Christmas may be particularly difficult; for Americans, Thanksgiving, and so on.

There are three solutions. The first is simply being aware, painful though it is, that what one is going through is normal in the sense that everyone goes through it. This gives a sense of order and predictability to the situation and a sense that it is possible to get through it since others have. Recognising the feelings for what they are gives some sense of control and also a way of talking to others about the situation. It takes little effort to explain one's miserable countenance in terms of 'homesickness' or something similar since others will understand if they have been around for long enough.

The second solution is to keep going despite how one is feeling. A particular feature of any form of depression is the tendency to withdraw and so reduce the opportunity to be drawn out or to experience pleasure. Keeping going means that one has increased opportunity either to put 'home' in context or to have one's feelings of despair lifted by positive experiences. Keeping going physically also tends to stimulate the body's particular biochemical forces which are associated with positive feelings and thus encourage one to do more.

The third solution is to allow oneself to be homesick for a chosen limited period but either in private or with others from the same background. Here we are not thinking of a 'pity party' tempting though that can be but perhaps a chance to celebrate 'home' for what it is – a good place, a long way away.

Anecdotally it is always suggested that having a good sense of humour helps to alleviate the adjustment phase. No studies have been done to examine that idea although at a common sense level it seems to ring true. Certainly humour, and particularly a predisposition to humour, can be immensely helpful. The danger is that humour can act as a form of denial defending the team member from getting in contact with the perception of 'differentness' about the culture. Foreign cultures, as seen above, are not simply the same as our own culture with a few differences here and there. Rather they are quite alien in their world view, values and resultant behaviour and the process of engaging with the culture has to recognise that at both a rational and a feeling level.

Humour is invaluable if it includes the ability to laugh at one's self and one's mistakes. Other cultures are as used as we are to the idea of 'stupid (i.e. inept) foreigners'. Foreigners make mistakes and, by and large, that is fine by the host culture if the foreigner is willing both to learn from the mistake and not take themself too seriously. Errors are forgiven and everyone can have fun learning.

A colleague was living in Romania shortly after the events of 1989. There were still food shortages and shops tended to stock the same sort of items for extended periods of time. Queues were long and stocks could be sold out even whilst one was waiting. On one occasion she was queuing for meat. Beef had been the sole meat on sale for some weeks and so she was well used to negotiating with the shopkeeper about buying it. As she got to the front of the line she spotted what could only be lamb joints alongside the beef – but could not remember the Romanian for lamb. She was well known in the shop and greeted accordingly by the shop keeper who expected her to ask for her usual supply. Thinking quickly my colleague smiled and calmly asked for "2 kilos of 'baaaa' ". The incident brightened up everyone's day, she got a good deal on the meat -- and has the Romanian for lamb indelibly etched on her memory.

Resolution of the adjustment phase is developing the ability to hold the foreignness of one's living situation in tension with the loss of familiar home comforts. For some people it is possible to point to a particular instant where they 'knew' they had emerged from the adjustment phase. For some it is on waking on a particular day, for others a dawning realisation that they can cope and that the 'darkness' is behind them. Certainly the normative experience is for the resolution to happen over a brief period of time, sometimes an apparent instant, sometimes a few days.

There are a number of things to note about the resolution phase. Perhaps the key thing is not expecting to recover one's apparent 'first love'. That is fortunate – it is simply not possible to live life at such a level of intensity for long. However, for some, this phenomenon can cause doubts along the lines of asking if they are 'losing their call' or whether they are 'really' cut out for a particular culture.

The resolution is not permanent or smooth sailing. One can still have bouts of homesickness but these tend to centre around specific events or issues rather than being an overwhelming feeling of everything being wrong. The following is speculative but it follows from Kwast's 'onion rings' model (above) that there will be a continual stream of adjustments to be made. Major ones will occur as one moves from behaviour at home to behaviour in the host culture. After that will come an adjustment as one encounters different values or beliefs and then adjustment as one encounters the host culture's world view. The dynamic, of course, is not as cut and dried as that. Within each of the rings one may be encountering all sorts of different ideas which need to be accommodated.

From the above it would seem, in the absence of thorough investigation, that there tends to be a major crisis for most people which centres around adjusting to a different culture in the first place. That adjustment is more akin to mourning the loss of one's home culture than anxiety about engaging the host culture. Following that may well come a series of 'mini' (but still intense) crises centred around either specific events at home such as the way to celebrate anniversaries or specific cultural encounters as one becomes more familiar with the host culture.

B. Re-entry adjustment

'Coming home' is difficult since, for many people, it may not be like coming home at all. One felt 'at home' overseas. Although Foyle[11] has not commented it seems logical to assume that the re-entry process is also akin to a mourning or grieving process.[12] The dynamics involved in returning are complex but, from the work of our department over the last six years with many hundreds of returned workers, there seem to be five very common reactions. We have labelled them isolation, guilt, spiritual, health and 'premature return'.

(i) Isolation

This key dynamic is usually due to the intensity of the overseas experience, particularly if short term. Returnees are no longer the same as they were when they went out. They will be more or less inspired, disillusioned, passionate, defeated, hopeful. They will have found a new way of being which does not necessarily fit well with their home culture. Many will have identified with the host culture in some way in terms of dress, hair style, body language and so on.

Humour, even if grim, at this stage of the re-entry process is vital. Knowing that those about to greet returnees are almost bound to say something daft helps as well. In debriefing we often generate a list of the sorts of things that those returning have been greeted with. The following are typical:

Did you have a nice time dear? (to a refugee camp worker)

You're not very brown.

Gosh, you haven't changed a bit (to a worker overseas for ten years).

How was Malawi? (To a Mozambican worker).

Nice to see you, How was Rwanda? Now I must tell you all about Aunt Ethel's bunions.

Did you have a nice holiday?

Oh – been away then?

Did it work then?

Where do they begin? How do they explain? For those returning from a difficult place how do they contain themselves from telling their younger brother to 'eat his beans, there's people would be glad of them' without sounding either like their mother or a nag or both?

The almost universal dynamic that people experience is isolation. People simply do not understand and returnees are dimly aware that they cannot possibly understand. Yet it is the very people returnees want to understand whom they feel most isolated from. Family, friends, colleagues, particularly close friends no longer have the common understanding they once had. Because the overseas experience is precious and also because these people are precious returnees want to bring the two together – yet can't to their satisfaction. The result is a feeling of aloneness in the midst of the very people they assumed would both understand and with whom they have historically felt close to.

A more subtle feeling is that of no longer quite belonging. Not only do workers feel estranged from significant others, somehow they feel estranged from their home culture. The shallowness or coldness or insularity suddenly is no longer acceptable. There is a different way of doing things and, at this point, it seems better. Are the serials on TV really that important? Does the news reflect world affairs adequately? At the time of writing I have just spoken to a colleague spluttering at the end of the phone following an extremely harrowing field assignment. He complained vehemently that the news is full of a lone yachtsman rescued half way round the world and also the resignation of a football manager. Nothing is mentioned about any of the continuing half dozen wars in general or 'his' in particular.

The alienness goes deeper however. Nouwen *et al*[13] said that displacement was people gathering together away from the ordinary and proper way of life and finding a new way of being together. Whilst overseas, aid workers and missionaries have found new ways of being. For the diplomatic corps 'going native' is the worst thing one can do. For the missionary and the aid worker it is often essential. One becomes enculturated. What that actually means though is that one feels incompetent in at least two cultures. One never fully takes on the culture of the host nation unless one goes there as a child. Equally one never totally loses one's home culture although significant parts of it may be lost.

The result can be what Christ described as 'having nowhere to lay my head'.[14] For the Christian we are 'strangers in a strange land', 'a pilgrim people'. It sometimes takes travel to a different culture to make this clear to us. Not only did we never fit totally in the host culture, not only do we not now fit 'back home' but also, as Christians, we do not fit truly into this world at all. The pessimistic way of describing this is to become preoccupied with aloneness and not feeling truly at home anywhere. The optimistic way of describing the phenomenon is to feel the sense of being a 'world Christian' – at home no where in particular but able to settle anywhere. The 'right and proper place' has gone – forever.

Isolation is also heightened by the particular form of conversational style we adopt in the west. Basically, particularly for men but also for women, we use competitive story telling as a conversational device. In conversation, by and large, my job is to tell an entertaining story. My conversational partner must then tell a marginally better story which it is then my job to cap. The one forced to change the subject loses.

Part of the hassle of dealing with returning missionaries is that competitive story tellers know they are on to a loser right away. It doesn't matter what their opening gambit is, the missionary is bound to be able to cap it immediately and, in so doing make the listener feel instantly inadequate. Better by far, then, to avoid the missionary since the story teller believes they have nothing to contribute to the conversation.

An equally subtle problem is the guilt of those who feel they have been left behind. One week the missionary was the same as them; house, mortgage, cat, elderly parents, children and some church ministry to support. Suddenly, it seemed, the missionary was writing incredible letters home from somewhere that might feature on the evening news any day now. How did it happen? However it happened those who have been left behind feel vulnerable. They can feel that they have no excuse not to do similar things, yet they feel unable to summon the courage to change. The missionary returns and those who stayed at home avoid them.

Many delightful experiences can follow which give clues to some of the solutions for feelings of isolation. On my first trip back to my home church after joining YWAM I was approached by an elderly lady whom I had never spoken to before. She took me by the arm to a corner of the entrance hall away from others and, with tears in her eyes, said 'I'm so delighted you have gone. You see I had my call 60 years ago but I met my husband and life moved on. I could have gone but didn't and I've regretted that ever since. I'm so pleased you've been obedient, I'd hate for others to do what I did'. She walked away at that point but she and I had understood each other at a very deep level. She remains one of our most faithful prayer supporters.

Companionship is not necessarily generated by returning to those who are our historic companions. Rather it is generated by being with those who share common vulnerabilities. Returning missionaries and aid workers normally have most in common with those who are also returned missionaries and aid workers. Age, profession and location of service are irrelevant. It is sufficient to have experienced another culture at more than a trivial level and to have found one's own culture wanting.

(ii) Guilt
There are two forms of guilt – guilt at leaving the field and guilt at being 'home'. The first form of guilt centres on that which has been left behind.

> 'Who will be looking after x now I am away'?[15]
> 'I feel so bad that I can leave and they can't'

Such feelings can be further intensified when the departure has been involuntary.

The second form of guilt focuses on the obvious luxury and convenience of the everyday experience of being back in the West: being able to get drinking water from a tap, go shopping and so on. One particularly intense form can be the 'supermarket' experience or the 'return to work experience' where the choice, variety, size and abundance can be overwhelming. Often returning aid workers do well in a supermarket until they hit the pet food aisle. There is no harm in having pets (although the average daily cost of keeping a pet alive can be more than that spent keeping a refugee alive) but the choice of food can seem obscene, particularly when the diet dog or cat food is spotted.

An entirely normative reaction then can often be the reluctance to spend money, or have money spent, on apparently frivolous items. Having one's own car, going to the cinema, hiring a video can all provoke guilt. The 'welcome home' party is a charming thought but – to quote Judas – the money would surely be better spent on the poor. We live in the tension between two worlds – and have to learn to live with that.

The dynamics underlying guilt can be complex and intense for some time. In some ways they may never fade and that may not be a bad thing. For me my frequent memory jogger about overseas is simply turning on a tap. In my time I have turned taps on and seen nothing come out or seen a highly polluted fluid come out or not had a tap available. In the west turning on a tap for me can quickly turn my mind to prayer for those less fortunate. Despite the joy of having a young son the emotions involved in going round one particular supermarket devoted to toys can at times be intense. The obscenity of the abundance of trivia is overwhelming – and yet again I am prompted to pray for the poor in the midst of injustice.

Other forms of guilt may also be present, particularly if one is dependent on supporters or if the expectations of the agency have not been fulfilled.

(iii) Spiritual

Re-entry can also be a time of intense re-evaluation of one's personal theology. God may be viewed as good and generous, faithful and sure. He may not. Either way the theology that sufficed up to the time of departure somehow no longer does so. One returnee visited a colleague and me to talk through the two Christian Gods she observed. Her return was at the height of the 'Toronto Blessing' in the UK and she perceived that one God had middle class suburbanites falling over and laughing at the least prompting. The other God apparently failed to answer prayer in the face of unremitting poverty, injustice and hopelessness in an African city. Is the God of suburban England the same as the God of urban Africa? The answer 'of course' was trite unless one had also felt the pain of the apparent difference.

These issues are covered more fully in chapter 7 and also below. It is however crucial to be aware that people's questions about God on return are often not academic in the sense of being of dispassionate interest. On the contrary, they are issues which people feel deeply and which need addressing sensitively and thoroughly. Chapter 7 gives an outline of some current thinking about the theology of suffering. It is difficult to know at what stage this should be taught. To do so prior to the overseas experience can seem a sterile exercise yet leaving such teaching until after the outreach can seem too late. On balance we teach the material prior to departure.

All the above issues can produce intense feelings of distress which are compounded by a very real lack of social and moral support. For those working with returnees it is helpful to emphasis the normality of their experience and that they are not going mad even though they may feel they are. Where possible it is also helpful to outline the sorts of processes that they are likely to experience which gives them some notion of the orderliness of the process they are in and courage to face the future.

Keeping things in perspective seems key – Luke 10 v 20 – 'do not rejoice at what you did, but that your names are written in heaven'. In other words God is less interested in our actions than in our relationship with Him.

(iv) Health

Issues of physical health may need to be addressed. Somehow returnees need to get the message that any illness, particularly fever, needs medical attention and that the attending medical staff need to be given information about recent (i.e. up to a year) overseas trips. It is not uncommon for returnees to bring back some form of infection which is very straightforward to treat by a tropical disease specialist. The message is a simple one yet oddly difficult to get across. Returnees seem to be a stoical bunch by and large and will ignore many physical symptoms or simply trivialise them rather than get the help they need to cure the underlying problem.

(v) Premature return to the field

There is a final phenomenon that only affects a minority of individuals but is quite intense. We have nicknamed it affectionately the 'Kate Adie syndrome' in recognition of the exploits of the chief reporter for the BBC. Ms Adie has appeared regularly on the BBC from the hotspots of the world and her reporting has been outstanding in the clarity with which dramatic events have been reported under enormous pressure. Of particular note was her report from the front lines of the allied troops just prior to the start of 'Desert Storm' during the Iraqi conflict. The Independent has carried a cartoon showing Kate Adie in front of the four horsemen of the Apocalypse with the caption 'This is Kate Adie for the BBC at Armageddon'.

For many British aid agencies there is both a formal and a (humorous) informal withdrawal criteria in the face of danger. The first is the well recognised one of withdrawing if Medecins sans Frontieres withdraw since MSF will only withdraw both if everyone else does and only if the team is under enormous threat. The second, informal, withdrawal criteria is the arrival of Kate Adie in town.

We suggest that there are missionaries and aid workers who find it next to impossible to function at home. Life is too dull and they long for the thrill of overseas work. After a short while at home they flee back overseas. No studies have been conducted in this area but the hypotheses are obvious – some people are only able to find their identity in dangerous or troubled situations. (The often heard remark 'I'm only alive when overseas' perhaps provides the best anecdotal evidence for this). Our identity is in Christ and not in our activities yet, for many, the thrill of helping in the midst of danger helps them to find an apparent identity or purpose. As with any addiction, however, the intensity of the fix must continually increase and so expeditions of increasing duration and danger are undertaken.

In training overseas workers and also in receiving them back we suggest that boredom at home coupled with the memory of the thrill of overseas work does not constitute a 'call'. The call of God is not to be found in the earthquake, wind or fire but in the still small voice which comes from a place of peace. It is that peace which we encourage people to find before they even consider returning abroad.

3) TEAM DYNAMICS

The centrality of this topic to the success or otherwise of a team cannot be overemphasised. To me it seems that the very heart of Christianity and the best practice of modern psychology meet here.[16] When thinking about teams from a purely Christian perspective it seems best to think less in terms of team dynamics and more in terms of a community reflecting the Body of Christ incarnationally. To that end I have found the work of Henri Nouwen and colleagues[17] very helpful. Apart from his extended bible study on Philippians 2, four other passages are also of particular note – Micah 6:8, I Corinthians 13: 4-7, Galatians 5:22 and Ephesians 4:26.

There are a number of points which psychology can offer in this area. The Myers-Briggs[18] approach to personality assessment provides probably the most accessible and robust approach to understanding individual personality differences and, through that, an understanding of the commonest tensions within teams. Recent insights from the study of psychological trauma help us to understand the necessary components of leadership and of team life. Finally what I have called isolation factors, those things which draw or repel us to or from one another, are also of immense value.

The value of the above is threefold. First they are extremely straightforward to teach and the material can usually be covered adequately in less than two teaching hours for those going overseas for a brief period and up to a teaching week (say 12 hours lecture time maximum) for those going for longer. The material tends to resonate both with workers who have not yet been overseas and particularly with those who already have some overseas experience. Finally the material is readily applied on the field and appears to make a difference at least by virtue of giving people a common vocabulary and set of values by which to work.

A. A theology of teams

Let us consider first some of the theology underlying 'teams'. Nouwen et al do an extended bible study on the well known Christological passage in Philippians 2:1-11. One of their key themes is the way in which Christ is revealed in Christian community. Their definition of community is as follows:

'Forming community is to move away from the ordinary and proper place and be gathered in displacement (e.g. Luke 14:26, 9:60,62; 18.22)'[19]

They note that the Greek components of 'ecclesia' or church imply 'being called out' much more than 'being huddled together'. Being called out is a perpetual call, not a one-off call. We can see this clearly in Philippians 2:6-8 where Paul describes Christ being called from Heaven to earth and from there to death on a cross.

We can expand this further by looking at the life of Christ as a whole. Indeed Christ is called from Heaven to Bethlehem (to a family itself in displacement). From there he becomes a refugee in Egypt. On His return to Nazareth He is called to an itinerant ministry. Just as that is becoming established he is called to displace himself further, to a triumphal entry into Jerusalem followed by His death. His death is total, that is to say He is further displaced from the Father's very presence to 'the dead'.[20] From there he returns to earth and is then displaced back to Heaven. Astoundingly, to me at least, His displacement does not end there. At the end we do not go to Him, He comes to us.

The ordinary and proper place that Nouwen and colleagues refer to is difficult to define. It is not a geographic location but rather an attitude to life or understanding of God's purpose in our lives. As they say, 'In moving away from the ordinary and proper place we lose the illusion of having it together'.

For me my 'call' to YWAM was unexpected. In praying it through I was initially clear that my professional skills would best 'serve' God in the English speaking world, logically the south east of England where I come from. It took some time before it dawned on me that I really couldn't restrict God's call in this fashion. My wife and I then worked for a little while in a non-English speaking part of the world before we understood more of the nature of our call. When it came I was embarrassed – it was to a YWAM centre in the south east of England, not even twenty minutes drive from our home church. I could not believe that I had joined a worldwide organisation only to end up on my front door step. Yet I was also conscious that I was in this part of the world on God's terms not mine. Perhaps that for me is a good working definition of being displaced.

So – why did God displace himself? – Nouwen *et al* put it well: 'So that nothing would be alien to Him and so he could fully experience the brokenness of our human condition. If we are to follow Christ then it seems that we must not be alienated from those we seek to serve, we must, in some way experience their brokenness'.

The Christian community gathers together in displacement and, in so doing, discovers and proclaims a new way of being together. It does not gather together out of shared anger, anxiety or economic necessity, although there are undoubted economic benefits to living in community, but rather to make the presence of Christ manifest.

Several other points need to be made. Displacement is not a goal in itself, it is meaningful only when it gathers us together in a new way. In being displaced we meet people with similar needs and struggles and so meet together with a common vulnerability. By being vulnerable we do not set out to displace ourselves so that we are perceived as especially unique or outstanding.

Nouwen *et al* then go on to describe the necessity of 'disappearing as an object of interest'. Taking Philippians 2:3 as their starting point they point out the need to move away from being the focus of the attention of people and, instead, to focus on how to be more Christ-like. As we focus on that our concern then becomes how to be present to people in a Christ-like way. In the words of the classic hymn, 'It's no longer I that liveth but Christ that liveth in me'. As we 'disappear' so people's attention is more clearly drawn to Christ.

An illustration I like to use is that of a common game used in Christian circles called "Angels and Mortals". For a period of time, usually a week to a month, each person in a group is assigned another person, called an angel, by lot. The angel's task is to look after their 'mortal' during this period by praying for them regularly and perhaps sending them small presents or messages of encouragement. Part of the fun of the game is for the angels to try to preserve their anonymity during the period of the game. This brings me to my point. Often, at the conclusion of the game, the mortals want to know who their angels are in order to thank them. It is not at all uncommon for the angels to be happy for their identity to be revealed in this way and then to bask in the, brief, adulation that follows. Disappearing as an object of interest in this context would be being prepared to have your identity as an angel remain a secret.

Jesus made the point more strongly in Matthew 6 vs 2-6; let your giving and praying be in secret. Those who do give and pray publicly have already received their reward. To do otherwise can also get in the way of people praising God for their present good circumstances or blessing. If they are so busy thanking and praising people then there may not be space for them to praise God to whom the praise rightly belongs.

It comes as no surprise to the Christian that it is not the outward behaviour that is important here but the inner motivation. If the purpose of our service is to be praised ourselves then it is worth nothing in eternity. If the purpose of our service is to see God glorified then it is worth everything. Interestingly we may still receive the praise of people but that will be secondary to the praise people give God. Christ found favour with people yet continually pointed the way to the Father.

It follows then that a key dynamic within a team is self-sacrificial service. This is not to be confused with workaholism or the kind of behaviours which lead to burnout. Rather our service should seek to bless and build up others rather than seek to puff ourselves up. (Phil 2:3). We lose the 'look at me' mentality so familiar in the 1980's and gain instead a 'look at Christ' mentality.

Self-sacrificial service has a tendency to be confused with pathetic or spineless behaviour. The current Pope[21] has used a phrase – the omnipotent powerlessness of Christ – to outline the dynamic involved. Christians are not to be 'meek' in the face of adverse conditions. The God we serve is a God who has chosen to limit His omnipotent power – as a result He loves even us and calls us to love even those who harm us. That may sometimes involve us remaining silent in the face of personal injustice as Christ Himself did before Pilate. It may involve us speaking out for justice as Paul did when he claimed the rights of a Roman citizen. Wisdom, in servant-hood, is knowing the difference.

Teams of Christian workers are therefore gathered in displacement away from the individual member's ordinary and proper place. Each member is seeking to disappear as an object of interest and to have the same attitude as Christ through their thoughts and actions. (Phil 2:5). The attitudinal changes involved above are profound and, to me, seem only possible as a work of Grace.

B. A psychology of teams

I have found it has been salutary to see the way in which much of modern psychology follows the theology outlined above. Let me say immediately that I do not need psychology or any other 'ology' to validate Christian theology. However, I subscribe to the view that there is a 'really real' reality out there and that the reality is based on God's laws or rules in Creation. To me it doesn't matter what background the 'ologist' comes from, reality is simply there to be discovered and it is inevitable that psychology will become at least consistent with what God says about how we should live our lives.

Two recent developments in psychology have outlined the necessary components of a team which preserve its integrity when under extreme stress. The technical terms are 'cohesion' and 'consultative leadership'.

'Cohesion' is the ability of team members to give and receive affection. Perhaps another way of putting it would be the pleasure of the team in one anothers' presence outside of their working relationship.

Periodically, as part of my work, I am asked to travel to see a team which is not doing so well. Part of my assessment is to watch the team at play rather than at work. It is particularly instructive to see how they handle the boundary of recreation and work. Most teams I visit have scheduled meetings of one form or another. I begin to think the team may be in trouble if I am in the room set aside for the meeting a minute or two ahead of schedule and no one else is there. Team members then begin to arrive but the atmosphere for the troubled team is one of getting down to business as quickly as possible. At the scheduled time for the meeting to finish, the team leaves en masse for 'essential' duties elsewhere. I am left alone in the room wondering why the team has no joy in one anothers' presence, even to the extent of lingering for a few moments to chat to one another.

Later in the day comes lunch or some other meal. I enjoy my food and so usually contrive to be well on time for scheduled meals. I know the team is in trouble if, again, I am the only one at the mealtime a few moments ahead of schedule. The meal time can feel very much like an eating task rather than a chance to be with colleagues or friends. On finishing the eating task, the team disperses. There is no cohesion, no joy in one anothers' presence for the sake of it. No fun.

This self same team will, in all probability, do a good project. They will plant churches, drill wells, dispense medicine, even develop communities or empower the poor. Under stress however, they will do badly and, under extreme stress, individuals are considerably more likely to become traumatised.

Currently the research evidence for that consists of retrospective studies. However there are some psychological theories which would predict much the same phenomenon. The key theory is that of 'Social Support'. It has been well documented for some decades that friendships outside the immediate family are central to mental well-being and, indeed, physical well-being. The nature of these friendships is defined as intimate, in the sense of self-disclosure of intimate information; confiding (i.e. trustworthy) and reciprocal. A reciprocal friendship is one where both partners claim friendship with the other and are mutually supportive. It seems that the nature of the network of friendships is also key. The size of the network is of less importance than its density. By density is meant the extent to which the friends in a network know one another and also claim friendship with one another.

The second key element is that of the leadership style. For leadership to be protective during times of stress it must have the quality of being willing to consult. The dynamic is a subtle one. It does not mean a democracy where there is a referendum on every activity. It is more the ability of the leader to have a clear approach but a willingness to have that approach discussed or even challenged. In that way the people following the leader buy in to the decision making process and feel both empowered by the process and also that they have bought in to the eventual outcome. Non consultative leaders produce teams who become stressed under pressure and who are more likely to become traumatised under extreme pressure.

From the above it should be clear that becoming stressed is less to do with the nature or intensity of the stress and more to do with the nature of the support individuals feel they have when being stressed. From that it follows that putting teams together which are cohesive and who have leaders who are willing to consult will do well in times of stress or trauma and that the reverse is also true.

As I have considered these aspects it has seemed to me that they map onto some basic Christian truths which are well known. Cohesion can be thought of equally well in terms of fellowship (1 Corinthians 13, the 'one another' verses in the New Testament and so on). A consultative leadership style maps on to a deeper truth – that of servant leadership for whom Christ is our central example.

In thinking about teams it is helpful to give team members tools to understand some basic team dynamics and thus an insight into potential team conflicts and their resolution. The two most helpful that we have found are an outline of the Myers-Briggs Type Indicator (MBTI[22]) and a model of the natural history of teams.

For some teams it may be possible for them to do a full Myers Briggs Inventory as part of their induction. For other teams it may be sufficient for them to have a working knowledge of the approach so they have a common vocabulary with which to describe differences and similarities amongst themselves. The MBTI posits four basic personality traits. These are:

introversion(I)/extroversion (E)
sensing(S)/intuitive(N)
thinking (T) feeling (F)
judging (J) /perceiving (P).

Everyone is considered to be either introvert or extrovert, sensing or intuitive and so on. Thus people will tend to fall into one of sixteen categories – e.g. ISTJ, INTP, ENFP and so on.

The definition of each category is complex but some working definitions are sufficient for team members to get enough of a flavour of the MBTI for it to be useful.

For the MBTI, introversion and extroversion are less to do with party going behaviour or its absence and more to do with how we "refuel" and how we process information initially. When resting or relaxing, introverts tend to prefer isolation or solitude. Curling up with a book or going for a long walk on their own is refreshing. By contrast extroverts find being with other people helpful when relaxing. When tired they like to seek out others with whom to relax. Mixing introverts and extroverts in dormitory accommodation over a long period of time can be immensely character building for the individuals involved – one group will wish to be quiet when in 'their' bedroom. The other group, should they ever come to the bedroom other than to sleep, will want to invite other people in or tell their room-mates at length about their day. These contrasting dynamics interfere dramatically with the introvert's ability to get on with writing their personal diaries and the extrovert's ability to think aloud.

Conversational style is quite different. Extroverts tend to think out loud and also to talk at the same time as other people. They will tend to keep talking until interrupted. Once interrupted they will keep quiet only long enough for another idea to occur to them which they will then immediately want to offer to the conversation. Introverts on the other hand process ideas in their heads and, in conversation, wait patiently until there is a natural gap into which to place their well formed thoughts. If interrupted they will fall silent in order to process what is being said to them. Extroverts find introverts frustrating as the introvert tends not to interrupt or contain them. Introverts find extroverts frustrating because they feel they cannot get a word in edgeways.

The distinction between sensing and intuitive is the way in which information is processed and handled. Sensing types tend to prefer details and facts, intuitive types prefer to consider the broad picture and to think conceptually. On one occasion my wife and I were out with a friend. Of me it has been said that I wouldn't know a detail if it hit me in the face. My friend, however, is very at home with detail and enjoys factual information in common with my wife. It was at the time of the Russian President Yeltsin's first serious heart attack. During the conversation my friend asked me how the ailing president was doing. I enthusiastically launched into a five point lecture on the state of the Kremlin, the likely outcome of three different scenarios and the international implications of all the above. Halfway through the first subheading of my second point my friend lent over and quietly said – 'I just want to know if he's dead'. Since then the incident has become a useful standing joke and my friend only has to say 'Yeltsin' to immediately stop me being inappropriately long winded (i.e. to talk about facts not concepts). Alternatively I can ask if she wants the 'Yeltsin version' in response to a question, i.e. to talk conceptually.

The third pair of MBTI items is 'thinking' and 'feeling', that is the way in which decisions are processed. For 'Thinkers' the principle is what matters. They will tend to come to conclusions based on logic and practical outcome. For 'Feelers' more of a situation ethic can appear to apply. They will tend to come to decisions which keep the peace and with which everyone is happy. They are good at getting consensus but may shy away from making a principled decision if that might offend people.

The fourth and final pair of items is 'Judging' and 'Perceiving'. Decisions can also be processed in terms of information gathering or in terms of getting to closure. For judging people achieving closure is more important than the quality of the decision. The quality of the decision is of less importance than the fact that a decision has been made. They would hold that if the wrong decision is made then it can always be changed. By contrast perceiving types will hold off making a decision until they think they have all the information to hand. They will be reluctant to close a decision in case further information comes to hand or in case it closes off other possibilities. They will be concerned that the right decision is made. For judging types their motto might be to get the ship out of harbour and get moving so the thing can be steered in the light of changing circumstances. For perceiving types their motto might be not to let the ship leave harbour without consulting all the charts first and then drawing up a navigation plan that is right.

In MBTI theory maturity is not one particular type but rather the ability to respond appropriately given the situation. During a written exam one cannot be an extrovert, during a party it is simply rude to introvert and so on.

For those used to thinking in MBTI terms many potential conflicts or misunderstandings can be circumvented simply by people commenting using MBTI terms about the underlying dynamics of a situation. Thus someone could comment during a strategy meeting that 'we need to be a bit more J about all this' or 'you are being quite P about this decision' and so on. In team settings after a trying day people may say that they need 'to introvert' or 'to extrovert' for a while. Their colleagues know what they mean and are freed up to give them the appropriate space.

C. The natural history of teams

Giving people an understanding of the stages teams tend to go through helps in two ways. It gives team members some understanding of the types of processes they may experience which thus affords some degree of predictability. It also gives people a working vocabulary to describe the process or which they can use to talk about the process to others.

Several models are available but the one we tend to use follows that of the cultural adaptation model since the two often complement each other.

Four phases are described – the honeymoon, adjustment and resolution phases and then endings. Some consideration is also given to conflict and its resolution.[23]

The 'honeymoon' phase is actually quite inaccurately named. Sometimes it is indeed characterised by an apparent idyll. However that analysis is quite shallow. It is better thought of as three separate but inter-linked dynamics – our tendency to try to impress in the early stages of any relationship, our unconscious first impressions of other people in the early stages of a relationship and our sense of relief at having 'made it'. For most people the need to 'find a friend' or ' be liked' or 'be respected' is strong and we will tend to be fearful that this may not happen during the early stages of team life. The result is a tendency for new arrivals to 'be on their best behaviour' in terms of doing things they imagine will make them attractive to others. Our initial impressions of others may tend towards feeling that they are better or more able than us and we may have an inner fear of not matching up to others' expectations. Again the tendency for the types of people who manage to get themselves selected for field service is to try to impress by living up to the perceived standards of the team or project.

The sense of relief at arriving can be profound, particularly for those on their first field trip. The relief can represent many things: the fulfilment of a life-long dream, the sense of success at simply having arrived after a rigorous selection process, the sense of hope that one's skills and dreams can finally be put to good use. One is energised, eager to get on with the task and to see things change. As a result there is often an apparent outward calm and pleasantness. Yet, underneath, individuals may feel quite fearful. They may feel that they should not have come and that they will fail to make it socially or professionally.

This fragile edifice comes to pieces during the adjustment phase. People cannot wear masks or be on their best behaviour all the time and eventually something has to give. What tends to give way are the trivial aspects of life – the amount of effort a colleague puts into work by comparison to their peers, the fact they monopolise some piece of equipment or have too many privileges, the amount of time spent in the bathroom or conversational styles. People simply start to irritate one another and the apparently happy atmosphere of the team can quickly degenerate into backbiting and quarrels. People have run out of energy to wear masks and now wish to establish who they really are.

The adjustment to all this can be complex and depends very much on the goodwill of team members to pull things back together and to accommodate one another. The process is one of being our real selves with one another. It is a key component of 'displacement' – to come together in our shared vulnerability and weaknesses rather than our perceived, neurotic strengths. Resolution comes when people realise they have need of each others' real strengths and yet are still acceptable to one another despite their weaknesses.

Shakespeare said that parting was such sweet sorrow.[24] In modern psycho-babble it is described as a complex dynamic. Some people find saying goodbye too painful and so go to great lengths to avoid it. Others feel comfortable at leaving. Much of this aspect of training is directed to the 'goodbye avoiders'. These people will find apparently valid excuses to leave prematurely and avoid any of the traditional farewells (final meal, graduation and so on). Yet those who are left behind can feel confused, angry or simply bereft that they did not have a chance to say their goodbyes to those who left prematurely. Saying goodbye is less about an act of departure and more about the chance, usually unrepeatable, to say those things that would otherwise be left unsaid. Some things are, in fact, best left unsaid but there are many things that are too difficult to say except under the pressure of a moment which may not be repeated. From that perspective we suggest that goodbyes are far too important to be left to the last possible moment of the last possible day. Rather there is a season in team life where goodbyes are possible. During that time there is opportunity to take time to appreciate team mates, colleagues from other agencies and local beneficiaries. Speeches and farewell meals are part of the process but they are not all there is to the closure process; taking time to have a final meal or drink with others to bring closure to one's role in the work or project are all part and parcel of saying 'goodbye'.

Leaders in particular need to be on the look out for what therapists call 'door handle' comments – those comments which are too difficult to say except with ones hand on the door handle and the chance to flee as soon as the comment is made. These comments can be both painful and positive.

Bringing things to closure during the 'goodbye' phase can be hard work. There may be a feeling of 'why bother' or 'only a few days to go' with accompanying feelings of either paralysis or helplessness. Team leaders have a crucial role during this period to make sure that people leave with as little unfinished business as is possible.

For long-term workers there is an additional phenomenon of perpetual bereavement. Working intensively in a team setting abroad and then leaving once in one's life is hard enough. Yet increasingly aid work and missionary work is characterised by repeated short or medium term service. After a while such workers find it increasingly difficult to summon up the energy to invest in new relationships when they know those people will move out of their lives in a short while. The response can be to refuse to invest in new relationships and simply to get on with the job in hand (a lack of cohesion) or to avoid the inevitable 'good byes'.

It is of marginal help to encourage career short termers to continue to invest in new relationships and it may be that this unwillingness to be bereaved yet again partly accounts for the high attrition rate of aid workers and missionaries. However there may also be some institutional solutions including the idea adopted by the military of setting up longer term teams to work on several projects rather than each project recruiting a completely fresh set of workers. (See Chapter 6)

D. *Conflict Resolution*

Several models exist and many agencies will have in hand some form of grievance procedure or policy. The fundamentals, however, are clear and straightforward when taken from a scriptural perspective. The first principal is one of due speed. Paul, writing to the Ephesians (4:26), commands people not to let the sun go down on their anger – in other words to settle disputes quickly. Matthew 18:15-17 outlines a procedure which seeks to minimise gossip and to bring resolution although it is principally aimed at resolving issues arising from sin.

Both principles need some expansion. Gossip needs to be minimised since it may affect both team morale and also peoples' perceptions both of the nature of the situation and the people involved. The idea implicit in resolution is that of restoring unity and less that of judging whether one person is right or wrong, vindicated, justified or whatever. The heart of the passage in Matthew cannot be understood from the modern Western perspective of an adversarial judicial and legal system which is concerned with judging which side is right and, by implication, which side is wrong. The essence of the bible message is reconciliation of relationships for the sake of the body of Christ.[25][26]

Essentially from Matthew we understand that we are, in the first instance to take our grievance to the one who has grieved us. If that does not bring resolution then other witnesses are to be brought. Failing that elders are to be brought in. If that fails then, difficult though it may be, leave the person alone. In modern parlance, walk away and 'get a life'. We find it difficult to do this as so many of us carry a deep need to be right or to be vindicated. This is not the way of Christ. We are justified through our relationship with Christ not through our relationships with other people. The gist of the procedure is therefore speed and resolution. Ordinarily disputes should be settled within a very short space of time or left behind so we can all move on.

People often ask at this point what happens if things are not settled. My advice is usually unequivocal. Leave. It may be that the dispute simply cannot be settled. It may well be that this solution is unfair, particularly if the 'aggrieved' party is the one to leave. However there is rarely anything to be served by continual in-fighting in a team, it certainly does not reflect the heart of Christ. People, both those who leave and those who stay, may then be freed up to get on with their ministry. I also subscribe to a 'free market' theory of team growth. Teams which are doing a good job and are cohesive will tend to attract further team members and retain them. Teams which are either doing a poor job or are dogged by personality conflicts or infighting will tend to have both a low recruitment rate and a high departure rate. However this can only be true if people do not remain in a dysfunctional team out of a sense of either misguided loyalty or (arrogant) belief that they can fix the situation given just a bit more time.

4) SPIRITUAL PREPARATION

For Christian teams going overseas a grounding in the basics of the theology subscribed to by the agency and some teaching on the practicalities of that are vital.

For short term teams the background and need for corporate Bible study, prayer and worship will need to be emphasised. In the time available over a weekend there is rarely more that can be done beyond outlining an apologetic for mission and God's heart for the poor and/or the lost.

Longer term teams require all the above topics plus a fuller treatment of missions. Additional topics would include character and nature of God, evangelism and, for those working with the poor, a good understanding of God's sovereignty and compassion. This latter section is given an extended treatment in Chapter 7. Each aspect of the Trinity would also be covered, in particular God's Father Heart, the person of Jesus, the Cross and Resurrection, the fruit and gifts of the Holy Spirit.

These topics have been written on extensively elsewhere. The purpose of teaching such things at this time is to give a firm foundation for the work that those being briefed are preparing for. A side benefit is the enhancement of the sense of community and of a sense of a corporate approach which will enhance teams' ability to function well. As those being briefed respond to the teaching and begin to live out what they are learning so the Spirit of Christ is made more manifest within them and they are able to reflect Christ more completely to the world around them. Despite the brevity of this section here, it is perhaps the most vital since it is from this base that the ministry of the team will flow.

5) PHYSICAL – HEALTH AND SECURITY

A thorough, reassuring, geographic specific briefing needs to be given. A number of excellent books exist on this[27] and the reader is referred to them. Typically the briefing will take the following form:

> The need for vaccinations and other prophylactics (e.g. malaria, vaccinations)
> The need for appropriate health and travel insurance
> An understanding of the sources of infection locally (e.g. running water, standing water, uncooked food, insects etc.)
> An understanding of how infection is transferred
> An understanding of what to do in the case of illness or emergency
> An authoritative but reassuring tour of the first aid kit and its contents.
> An outline of the agencies health policies with regards to, for example, AIDS
> A question and answer session.

The whole briefing need take little more than an hour accompanied by handouts. At the end people should feel realistically reassured about the health risks of their overseas assignment and empowered to act should anything happen. Participants should not leave feeling terrified and potentially paralysed by the dreadful diseases they may encounter but rather reassured that sensible precautions will help them avoid the majority of problems and that there are solutions for the majority of problems which do occur.

A thorough security briefing is also necessary as appropriate. Clearly this is required if going to areas of known danger and the briefing may need to be covered again on arrival as the local situation changes. Such briefings may also be required in areas which may be considered currently benign but which could develop problems. Participants may need to be made aware of routine precautions to be taken in certain areas. For example whether it is safe to travel at night, safe and unsafe modes of transport, particular areas to avoid, whether it is safe to wear jewellery and so forth. As with all training it is helpful to give more than just a list of do's and don't's, rather to spend time explaining the background to the issues involved.

6) AIMS AND OBJECTIVES OF THE TEAM
Stunningly this aspect of the work can often either be omitted, left so vague that it may as well have been omitted ('we're simply going to bless the local people in any way we can') or be unrealistic. Team members need to know why they are going and be given a 'warts and all' analysis of the probability of success. Team members need to be prepared for the very best laid plans not being followed through. Balanced against that is the old adage, 'If you aim at nothing you are sure to hit it'.

For those who prefer to think in cost benefit analysis terms a ten person team going from Europe to Africa for two weeks costs at least £7,000 and probably much more. For those working in Christian circles I had my first phone call from a pastor recently who had done the same sum. 'How can you justify the cost of this team given what they did'? was his quite reasonable question given the particular circumstances.

7) SPECIFIC SESSIONS
The outline curriculum for the majority of the sessions has been identified above. Additional specific sessions have also been included.

A. *Simulator*
As has been pointed out realistic training is required for those going into stressful settings. One of the best ways of doing that is through use of simulations – realistic, extended role plays of the dynamics that people will encounter. The most helpful forms at this stage of training are simulations which take people through some basic cross-cultural scenarios. Wycliffe Bible Translators have used a simulation called 'the Visa game' to great effect. YWAM has used a similar set up called the 'airport game'. In no way is the training intended to train people how to get visas or negotiate foreign airports, rather it exposes people to the realities of cross-cultural communication in a controlled way which then enables discussion and further learning to take place. An example is given in Appendix 2.

The heartfelt cry of the participants on first exposure to these simulations is an opinion that we are making things too tough and that life could never be so difficult overseas. On their return participants inform us gravely that the simulations are not tough enough.

One unintentional side effect of the simulations can be a difficulty for the participants to take aspects of foreign officialdom seriously. I was once in some far flung corner of the disintegrating Soviet empire trying to check in to a domestic flight in the 'foreigners' section of an airport. The convention at that time was to stand in a queue for the KGB, then for internal customs, baggage control and finally ticketing. I was the only foreigner checking in and had a large hall with the requisite four desks and accompanying scowling officials to myself. As I walked to the first desk the KGB officer walked off and busied herself elsewhere. After a wait of some moments it was but the work of an instant to convince her that I was not a significant threat to the (then) CIS. I walked past her to the next desk just in time to see that official also disappear. The officials at desks three and four had been trained to the same high standard of customer care and treated me in a similar fashion. I was unsure of the deep psychology behind all of this but was sure of one thing – I was having to bite my lip to stop myself from giggling at the thought that these officials must have been trained on one of our simulators.

B. Meeting with friends and relatives

A popular and much appreciated feature of YWAM's five day briefing for the year long teams is the involvement of parents, friends and relatives for the final session on the Friday afternoon. An overall presentation is made of the work of the agency in general and the work of the agency in each of the localities participants will be travelling to. An overview of the year is outlined in terms of training, work and locality. There is a condensed version of the teaching on culture shock and team adjustment. This is framed in the context of the type of letters friends and relatives may expect to receive – long and effusive to begin with, brief (though sometimes epic) and depressing after a while and then shorter and more distant as the extent of what needs describing becomes too much.

There is an extended period of questions and answers, usually concerning practical details followed by the chance to chat informally over tea. Representatives of the vast majority of participant's families and friends attend and are grateful for the chance to put the experience of their adult children or long standing friends into context and to have their questions answered.

[1] Three years undergraduate study then three years of bible school.
[2] Kwast in Winter R.D. and Hawthorne S.C. (Eds), *Perspectives on the World Christian Movement (Revised Edition)* Paternoster Press, UK, Carlisle, 1994.
[3] Lingenfelter, S.C. and Meyers M.K., *Ministering Cross Culturally*, Baker Bookhouse, Grand Rapids, 1986.

[4] These models are dated because of their static nature. Cultures are seen more dynamically in current anthropology. However the main thrust of teaching at this level is to portray the idea that cultures are different and to give some framework to predict that. For such a purpose these models are sufficient.

[5] Burnett, D., Clash of Worlds, Crowborough, MARC, 1995.

[6] David Bosch (1991) has written helpfully on this. In particular he takes 'modernity' and 'empiricism' to task for assuming the supremacy of their positions. As he points out, the latest way of doing things and the most scientific way of doing things are not, in fact, necessarily the best way of doing things. (Bosch, D., *Transforming Mission*, Orbis Books, New York).

[7] See also Elkins, P., Pay the Price, In O'Donnell and O'Donnell 1988 op cit.

[8] One church programme which went against the flow sent about $400 US each year to one family which fully funded one local adoption. At the time the average cost of illegally buying a child on the streets of Bucharest was over $1,000 US; the average cost of a legal adoption, overseas, of one child could run to well over $10,000 US.

[9] Wayne and Saly Dye together with Dorothy Gish have useful chapters covering the area in greater depth in O'Donnell and O'Donnell 1988 op cit.

[10] Lectures given 1994 onwards from unpublished research.

[11] Foyle ibid.

[12] Austin, C., has also covered this area in a Chapter 'Re-entry Stress: The pain of coming home' in O'Donnell and O'Donnell 1988, op cit.

[13] ibid.

[14] Mathew 8:28.

[15] And, yes, having such thoughts does indeed reflect on the extent to which our ministry was paternalistic, or not!

[16] A substantial section of O'Donnell 1992 op cit is taken up in consideration of this topic.

[17] Nouwen H, McNeill, D., and Morrison D.A., *Compassion*, London, Darton, Longman, Todd. 1982.

[18] *Myers Briggs Type Indicator*, Oxford Psychologists Press Ltd, 1997.

[19] Nouwen et al, ibid.

[20] Apostles' Creed.

[21] Pope John Paul II *Crossing the Threshold of Hope*, Jonathan Cape, London, 1994.

[22] op cit.

[23] The theoretical underpinning of this model owes more to psycho-dynamic theories than behavioural and can also be thought of in terms of the psychodynamic processes of 'beginnings, middles and endings'.

[24] Shakespeare, Romeo and Juliet, ii. 184.

[25] e.g. Colossions 3:14, Ephesians 4:3 and John 17:23. Other references exist to 'the ministry of reconciliation' (e.g.2 Corinthians 5:18) but these are to do with Christ's salvation rather than unity.

[26] David Cormack writes helpfully in 'Peacing Together' about the process of getting from conflict to resolution. (MARC, 1989).

[27] Lankester, T., *Good Health, Good Travel*. Hodder and Stoughton, London, 1995 and Aroney-Sine, C., *Survival of the Fittest*, MARC, Monrovia, 1994.

Chapter 4

Routine Debriefing

Friday, day one of debriefing: 'I've had it with missions', she said. 'I've come to this weekend to get rid of the rubbish but there's no way I'm going back out again'.

Sunday, day three of debriefing: ' Thank you' she said. 'I've got a whole heap of stuff into perspective now and I feel much more like talking to God about all of this'.

Today, four years later. Serving long term overseas.

YWAM Overseas Missions Manual:

Debriefing:
At the time of writing, debriefing for people returning from overseas service is still being established. In the UK it is routine for those ...[going overseas]. Debriefing weekends for those returning from long term service overseas are steadily being established.

What is included in debriefing?
Often the first thing to strike people after the first few days of being home is how isolated they feel. People don't really seem either to understand the joys and frustrations of life on the field. Worse, they may appear not even to care. Debriefing addresses these and other issues by giving sufficient time for people to:

- talk about their positive experiences to people who understand.
- talk through any feelings of isolation, disorientation, mourning, guilt, conflict resolution, etc., again to people who understand.
- be given practical help and guidelines for settling back and how to think about the future.

This type of routine debriefing is best done between a few weeks and two months of returning home. If, for some reason, you prefer not to be debriefed by YWAM or debriefing is not available then other organisations provide such services. Notably these are Care For Mission and Interhealth. Current addresses will be in the UK Christian Handbook.

(Taken from YWAM Overseas Mission Manual 1996).[1]

This chapter is primarily concerned with an account of the key dynamics involved in the psychological and spiritual debriefing of returning missionaries and aid workers. It is assumed that agencies have their own particular operational debriefing protocols and that the techniques described here would be supplementary to those. A detailed description of the procedures used by YWAM(UK) follows with respect to short term teams, students on courses including a short term field placement and long term individual staff members.

1. BACKGROUND ISSUES TO DEBRIEFING

There is little available literature to guide the principles of routine spiritual and psychological debriefing ('debriefing' hereafter). Many decisions about the methods we have developed have been based on practical considerations. For example, early on, we decided to debrief people in groups rather than individually. The practical reasons were purely the numbers involved. In any one year the department as a whole could be involved in the debriefing of 60 summer volunteers, 30 or more students returning from practical placements and a dozen staff returning from long term overseas work. It was simply not possible to debrief these numbers of people individually in a reasonable time.

The first types of teams to be formally debriefed were volunteers for short term practical placements overseas. As training courses were developed within the department so students returning from overseas practicums were also given extensive debriefings. With our growing confidence a service was then offered to staff returning from long term service (two years or longer).

We had to give careful thought to who actually did the debriefing. Put crudely the choice was between franchising debriefing out to another agency and keeping debriefing 'in house'. Within the UK there already exist excellent debriefing services, particularly for those who feel in some way damaged by their overseas experience. However such services generally debrief individuals and also come with significant financial costs. The relative tensions between confidentiality, internal feedback to the agency, freedom to share information and debriefer credibility needed thinking through which we did as follows.

If debriefing is franchised out then, inevitably, the issue of confidentiality needs considering. Generally debriefers who are independent of agencies primarily work for the individual or group coming for debriefing. As a consequence the agency will receive a more or less restricted report both on the individual and the situation they worked in from the independent debriefer. It is possible that the agency may receive no feedback at all. There may therefore be little effective feedback since the debriefer may be unaware of the full picture of what is being reported and the debriefer may also be unwilling to share the full picture with the agency for reasons of confidentiality.

To give an example, a colleague and I had been aware of a particularly difficult situation within a team on the field. We became aware of that over a period of time as staff returning from that situation reported similar dynamics. Whilst keeping confidence with the debriefee it has been possible to influence the situation. It seems to me highly unlikely that an external debriefing agency would be able both to pick up consistent themes and also act on them.

Debriefees may be more or less free to share information with an external agency rather than an internal debrief. In some ways the worker may be freed up to speak more emotively to an external agent than an internal one. They may also feel safer in speaking to an external person about hidden fantasies, doubts or worries than to an internal agent who may carry some influence over their future employment. By contrast it is considerably easier to speak to an internal debriefer who has at least some inside knowledge of the situations being spoken about.

Debriefer credibility is an important issue. Credibility may be a function of several factors. Probably the most important is the 'me too' factor – the notion that the debriefer knows what is being talked about because of their own personal experience. Two other factors also seem important. The first is the ability of the debriefer to hear what is being said accurately and without overly condoning or condemning the speaker. The second is the perceived ability of the debriefer to influence future events. In other words clients often hope that the debriefer will either be able to encourage current good practice where it exists or discourage bad practice where it exists. Credibility is agency independent for competent debriefers but, it seems to me, that there is an additional marginal benefit for in-house debriefing because of the perceived ability of the debriefer to influence practice or policy.

As a result of the above we have concluded that it is preferable to conduct debriefing in-house than to franchise it out. However we recognise the downside of the argument and encourage some individuals to go to independent agencies if that would benefit them more. We are aware that this is the sort of conclusion only a reasonably large agency could come to since smaller agencies may not have sufficient returning staff to justify employing a debriefer full time or even on a regular part time basis.

The solution adopted by many agencies of having the personnel officers debrief individuals or teams is an obvious one. The potential problem here is the perceived identification of personnel officers with 'management' and therefore the need for a degree of skill on the part of the personnel officer to get at potential problems.

An ethical issue for in-house debriefers is confidentiality. This needs careful working out and negotiating over a period of time and, it seems, is largely a matter of trust between the debriefer and the agency managers. Clearly debriefers are, more or less, employed by their agency and have a duty to report their findings to that agency. However many things are said in confidence to debriefers on an individual basis. This can range from an off the record style conversation where an individual may talk through some options prior to acting on their conclusions, through to confession of sin or loss of faith. Particularly after a trying time, many things can be said which really don't bear repeating and are more to do with ventilation than accurate feedback. At a crass level it does little for either party following such ventilation to feedback feelings of angst which may well be transitory.

Over the years we have concluded that our main duty of confidentiality is to the client or clients coming for debriefing. There are then two traps to avoid. The first is acting as a go between for clients and their managers where there is disagreement or misunderstanding. Our role is to help people clarify their thinking and encourage them to face situations themselves within their line management structure. I try to ensure that clients do not go back to their boss and begin the conversation 'Graham thinks that....' having had a number of incensed letters from leaders and pastors down the years following such an opening gambit by some clients!

The second trap concerns confession of sin or a perceived inability to function in missions or aid work by the client. The typical scenario is of an individual asking for a private conversation during a debriefing course following their perception that the debriefer is 'someone who will understand' or someone 'to be trusted'. In the course of the conversation it becomes apparent that their behaviour precludes them from service in the immediate future. Where does the duty of confidentiality lie? To me it seems still to lie absolutely with the client provided they are acting reasonably responsibly. I also find it helpful to make a distinction between temptations which are felt but still resisted (I feel tempted to steal project funds to pay my debts) from acted out temptation (I have stolen the project funds). In the first instance work needs to be done on the issues underlying the temptation. In the second instance work needs to be done on confession and restitution.

Perhaps we have been fortunate but in seven years dealing with sometimes quite serious situations my colleagues and I have never once had to break client confidentiality due to clients being reluctant to take their share of responsibility for the situations they find themselves in. (We have been inept and broken confidentiality once or twice by accident!) On the contrary we have been struck by how seriously aid workers and missionaries have taken their responsibilities in the process of debriefing, even to the extent of resigning. Mostly the solutions to apparently intractable problems have actually been very straightforward once the issues are considered objectively. At all times we retain a very high regard for the client's dignity and ability to choose. We insist that clients must follow through on the consequences of their behaviour since we are unable to do that for them.

Such a process however requires a high level of trust by the agency in the debriefing team's competence. In turn we find it necessary to be accountable to senior managers within the agency for our actions. In practical terms this could mean offering our own resignation should someone, for example, walk off with the project funds with our prior knowledge that this was a possibility, our judgement that the situation was contained and a decision not to inform relevant management.

2. CLIENTS PRESENTING FOR DEBRIEFING AND THE CORRESPONDING PROGRAMMES

There are broadly six categories of returning missionaries or aid workers:

1) Short-term volunteers who have gone out for the first or second time
2) Short-term volunteers who have been to the field more than twice with any agency
3 Students on courses which have an overseas practicum
4) Long-term staff (by definition those overseas for two or more years)
5) Volunteers or staff who are in crisis
6) Dependent children of missionaries (in the US the term is Missionary Kids or MK's).

Those who need to be seen due to a crisis are quite a separate category to the other groups and tend to be seen individually or in small groupings. The work with such clients is described in greater detail in chapter 6. Of concern has been recent unpublished research concerning the mental health of participants on short term teams in the months after their field trip. Using broad measures of mental health it was estimated that some 30% of participants would experience a transient depression sufficient to register on the relevant scales. Following Foyle it seems entirely possible that participants were experiencing an intense grief reaction following their foreign experience. It certainly lends support to the often heard comment from returning overseas workers that, in the months following their return they felt as if they were 'losing their grip' or ' going mad'.[2]

Three programmes have been developed to serve the groups who are returning home under routine or normal circumstances.

The first programme lasts between two days and five days and is designed for those who have been overseas for less than two years, in fact, usually less than one year. The programmes differ in length but the content is broadly similar. A number of different teams are typically debriefed together so participants will know a number of other people on the course but will also not know others so well.

The second programme is explicitly for long term missionaries and lasts two days. Participants in this course are usually strangers to one another and will have served for varying lengths of time, in different projects and different locations. This spread of background is valuable in helping participants to see the commonality of their return experience.

The third programme is run in conjunction with the second programme and is aimed at helping children of returning missionaries come to terms with, effectively, leaving home and moving to a very foreign country.

3. KEY DYNAMICS IN DEBRIEFING

Having been involved with debriefing some 700 people from a variety of experiences over the last six years it seems to me that there are a number of key dynamics available to the debriefer during sessions.

The first is the personal overseas experience of the debriefer or, what has been called 'credibility'.[3] It is crucial that this experience has been worked through to a large extent so that the debriefer is not caught up in their own history when listening to the stories of others. We encourage debriefers to make use of their experience of the joy and pain of overseas service and living conditions as they empathise with participants on courses. This then becomes part of the credibility of the debriefer. It becomes apparent to the debriefee that the debriefer really is able to understand the reality of what it is like 'out there'. The exercise is not sterile or academic but rather walking through the experiences with the debriefers and their co-debriefees as they come to a better understanding of themselves, their relationship with Christ and the recent past.

Ventilation is a well known dynamic in counselling. It is simply the chance to off load excess emotion without necessarily coming to a resolution. It brings at least transitory relief. For a healthy population it is very likely that ventilation will also quickly lead on to a resolution, particularly as so many of the feelings being spoken of are normative. In speaking about them people get the sense that others are in the same place and that, although intense, the feelings are quite valid and not to be feared.

A central quality of the debriefer then is possession of the skill of silence and a high tolerance of ambiguity and uncertainty. As a rough rule of thumb we suggest that debriefers speak 10-20% of the time during a session and that debriefees speak 80% of the time or at least have that time available after being given some careful questions to provoke thought. The aim is for the debriefees to make sense of their feelings by expressing what is going on inside or by hearing others express their feelings. The task of the debriefer is then simply to comment and validate what has been said.

To us it seems that healing takes place in a group as the participants realise they are going through a normal, shared experience. As we work with groups there is the continual sense of the healing or resolution happening 'out there' in the group rather than primarily in the interaction between the group and the debriefer.

It has become classic to the point of stereotype that groups will visibly relax as individual members pluck up the courage to say that they feel, for example, isolated. The debriefer need say nothing – in that instant both the courageous speaker and everyone else loses something of their aloneness.

For the above to work, however, participants need to be in a secure, safe, non-judgemental, affirming atmosphere. Typically towards the beginning of the first session of a debriefing programme participants will generate either positive comments or humorous comments with little content. After a while, usually after a silence, some brave soul will make some negative or derogatory remark about a minor problem. At that instant the debriefer has a chance to encourage further openness by homing in on their negative comments in an affirming way. The debriefer gives the debriefees permission to be horribly honest at the beginning of the session. The group experiments with being honest and the debriefer affirms them which keeps the openness coming, thus letting them work through their painful or joyful issues.

In this context, affirmation of debriefees 'bad' feelings means that the debriefer is taking notice, and the feelings can be validated by commenting, for example, 'that others go through that too'.

Extensive use is made of recording the progress of the debriefing sessions on flip-chart paper during the group debriefing. We have found that appropriate use of it will actually assist the debriefing of almost any sized group from four or five people upwards. The largest group we have used the technique with has been 60 short term volunteers.

The technique is straightforward. The debriefer generates a question such as "what sort of words would you use to describe 'coming home'". The debriefer writes the topic heading up and then continues to write as the group generates its answers. Usually, to the majority of questions, there are a rich array of comments and there are usually far too many for people to hold on to in their memories. Writing the answers up gives the group some sense of corporate identification with what is being said.

Generally the procedure seems to be containing for the group. That is, it provides a sense of safety for them and a sense that what they are saying will not be lost. When the group has completed what they want to share it is possible for the debriefer to comment on some of the issues that have come up and also to identify any themes that have emerged for the group. The key to the feedback is a process called 'normalising'. By and large the feelings and thoughts that returning missionaries and aid workers experience are remarkably similar and, in that context, may be called normal. Pointing this out produces immense relief for people for whom the thoughts and feelings were possibly powerful, unexpected, overwhelming and, subjectively, a threat to their mental health.

Groups tend to feel affirmed by the process. What is being said is important. Furthermore it is important enough to be literally noteworthy. In no way are the group's feelings or experience being belittled. On completion of each question the sheet of paper is put up somewhere indicating that we are continuing to consider the issues raised and have not just glossed them over or 'dealt with that one'.

For the debriefer faced by a large group of people the procedure gives some degree of control over the rate at which things are said. By and large the debriefer will try to keep pace but it is not an exercise in speed dictation and the participants will recognise that. As a result participants themselves will slow down and the pace of the debriefing will be much more measured.

A side benefit is that introverts have a chance to join in as well. The exercise, as described, is very much an extroverts paradise and introverts nightmare. It is entirely possible for introverts to join in as well by the debriefer asking silent (but willing to speak) debriefees which items they would endorse on the board and whether they have anything to add.

The other side benefit is that it helps to break up the process of debriefing into bite sized chunks. Several major issues may come up for people during the session and it is possible to construct an agenda whereby these issues can be explored further from what has been recorded on the flip chart.

By writing responses up it keeps the dynamics very public and helps participants to realise that the things they are going through are not uncommon.

A final point is that, for debriefers, routine debriefing after a while can become just that – routine. The same issues keep recurring and, although each group is subtly different, the underlying dynamics and issues can become predictable. It is therefore quite possible for the debriefing staff to lose contact with the immense amount of psychological energy that participants are expending in the process and the impact of the, sometimes intense, revelations they are experiencing. I vividly remember watching one participant finally hear a key point on overseas work. The fact the participant had learnt something was pleasurable for us as debriefers. The effect it had on the participant was quite devastating and he spent the rest of the session clearly stunned by the implications of several years of apparently misdirected ministry. In our eyes the point made was a tiny one and one we had taught many times – to the participant it was life changing. Debriefers need to stay alive to the very real power of debriefing programmes.

4. STRUCTURES OF ROUTINE DEBRIEFINGS

The rest of the chapter is given over to detailed descriptions of the various forms of routine debriefing carried out within YWAM (UK) since 1990.

Three forms of short term team debriefing outreach are considered and one form of long term debriefing. The three forms of debriefing short termers consists of those returning from a brief summer outreach programme, typically in sub-Saharan Africa (Impact Teams); those returning from a one year programme in a developing nation (Year For God) and course students returning from a twelve week practical overseas placement. Each programme typically will have people returning from many different locations. It is deliberate to debrief people from different teams together but within their programmes. This is partly for logistical reasons and also so that people can see that their experiences are common to all returnees not just those from a particular location or who have experienced a particular dynamic.

The Impact Team and Year For God participants will have returned home to family and friends for varying lengths of time prior to their debriefing sessions. For logistical reasons the students, typically, will be debriefed immediately on their return to the UK and will not have been home although most will have made at least telephone contact.

A characteristic of YWAM is the emphasis of people working in teams. It is extremely rare for people to serve overseas for any length of time on their own. Throughout the following, therefore, there is an emphasis on the debriefing of people within teams. For those used to debriefing individuals the group approach is still valid and the particular sections on teams are straightforward to remove.

A. Impact teams (Short term summer teams)

The debriefing of Impact Teams began in 1991 with summer teams returning from Romania and Africa. Attendance was sporadic even though several one day events were offered. As outlined in Chapter 3 the solution eventually was to offer the three phases of the programme as a complete package with debriefing a necessary part of the process as well as briefing and the outreach itself. Applicants signed up to all or none of the programme.

A programme which follows the standard procedures of Impact Team debriefing is outlined in Table 4-1. The introduction is partly logistical and partly a familiarisation with staff who will be taking part and also includes an outline of the programme. Upwards of thirty people can be present with forty or more participants not uncommon.[4] The participants represent teams of six to twelve people who have been to half a dozen locations for several months and who have now regrouped as a whole for the debriefing programme.

The content of the worship session, indeed its very presence, is always a risk. Team leaders by this stage will have reported back to the office about their work and some indication will have been given as to the perceived success or otherwise of the teams. By far the majority of people return with heartfelt thanks for their time overseas and a desire to express that. The worship, normally, is profound and there is a tremendous sense of freedom as people come together before God. It is also felt very appropriate to begin by praising God for who He is rather than waiting until some indeterminate time to praise Him for what He has accomplished. Nevertheless, care does need to be taken that an overwhelming number are not in a place where they would find it difficult to worship God because of a difficult outreach experience.

> **Table 4-1**
> **Example 'Impact Team' debriefing weekend**
>
> *Saturday*
>
> 11.00   Registration and refreshments
> 11.45   Introduction
> 12.30   Worship and thanksgiving
> 1.00   Lunch
> 2.00   Coming Home
> 3.30   Refreshments
> 4.00   Bible study
> 4.30   Debriefing of teams
> 6.00   Dinner and evening free
>
> *Sunday*
>
> 9.30   Worship
> 10.00   Team feedback with slides etc.
> 12.30   Futures
> 1.00   Lunch and home

Lunch is very much a time of participants catching up with each other by swapping stories. Interestingly many stories will be about coming home as much as reminiscing or telling members of other teams about their experiences.

The session on coming home is put in at this stage since people's frustration with the experience of returning is very much at the front of their minds. The session will easily take the full ninety minutes with the following being some typical questions used to get people to consider their feelings:

'What are some of the stupid things that have been said to you on your return'? (a humorous way of beginning the session – everyone has their horror story but, fascinatingly, there are rarely more than seven or eight stories which account for the entire group's experience).

'What words would you use to describe arriving home'?
'What words would you use to describe being at home'?
'What words describe the things you enjoy most about being at home'?
'What words describe the things you enjoy least about being at home'?
'What's been the most helpful event or circumstance since returning home'?

Some or all of the above questions can be asked. It is best by far to have your own set of questions, even better simply to go into the session and have a conversation with the group rather than going in with too many preconceived formulations. The aim of the session is to help people realise the commonality of their experience and the normality of it. None of these sessions are interrogations or simply information gathering exercises. The teaching that is given, where required, attempts to crystallise the information given by participants rather than following a set pattern or curriculum.

With that in mind the following represents the initial thirty seconds of feedback from one group of Impact Teams in response to 'What is it like to be at home'?

difficult, puzzling, nice, boring, isolated, frustrating, restful, flat, tired, excited, disappointed, anxious, out of place, bereft, upset, determined, angry, painful, guilty, sad.

The stream of thought slowed at that point and became more measured but it gave some indication both of the freedom people feel to express themselves and the pent up emotion that was present in a group of 20 year olds. Much of the expected dynamic was present and, as ever, the sense of relief began to flow as people realised they were not alone in the experiences they had been going through. The teaching from the front was simply a brief reminder of teaching they had already experienced. As the familiar overheads went up so the group was able to see the process they were in, to normalise it and begin to make use of it.

The Bible study is a chance for participants to pause and have input into their experience from a Biblical perspective. Again the type of input is going to vary widely depending on the nature of the teams and their shared experience.

Possibly the most tricky part of the debriefing comes with the debriefing of the individual teams. This is done in teams by staff familiar, preferably, with the location visited. Where there have been team problems then a staff member will be allocated with experience in conflict resolution irrespective of the specifics of their overseas experience. The time allocated is again up to ninety minutes although there is spare time in the evening if that is insufficient. However the evening time is only broken into reluctantly as that is seen as invaluable time for the teams to meet informally and relax. For a few this will be the first time they have been able to relax since returning home.

The potential content of the team debriefing is rich and it is rare to be able to cover all the aspects one would wish. Generally several principles need to be followed. Every person within the group has equal value – thus individuals should neither dominate nor be inactive. Each member should feel free to have their say confident that the information will not be repeated outside of the group setting.

Consideration needs to be given to covering the following topics:

The expectations of people for team life
Good aspects of the team
Not so good aspects of the team
Individual roles within the team
What people learnt from the experience of team life
Areas of conflict or disagreement and their resolution
Highlights of team life
'Lowlights' of team life.

How that is done is very much decided within the dynamic of the team itself and the individual debriefer. The typical experience of most teams and team members is excellent (remember that most will have operated well within the 'honeymoon phase' since their overseas experience was only brief) and the debriefer usually has more trouble containing the enthusiasm of the team than having everyone sitting in glum silence contemplating how awful everything was.

Care needs to be taken with enthusiastic teams that their enthusiasm is not a protective defence against the experiences of the field. One can be carried away with such teams and have the belief that everything is fine. Whilst defences are a good thing and need to be left intact, some prodding of them is valid to check whether people are in touch at all with the realities of what they saw. Becoming totally out of contact can be misleading for individual future career choices as people are drawn back to the fantasy of what they thought they experienced as opposed to the reality of what was actually there.

The evening is often a time for participants to begin showing photographs and reminiscing in earnest about their time overseas. Staff are not unwelcome but the conversation is full of 'in jokes' and reminiscences about tiny incidents and so are unlikely to feel that included.

Worship the following morning has less of a sense of relief or release about it and, usually, more of a sense of reverent thanksgiving for God's provision and a degree of intercession for His future provision.

The team feedbacks are then one of the few opportunities participants will have to present their work to a reasonably informed and supportive audience.

The concluding session concerns 'futures' and is usually a brief presentation of future opportunities with missions and other agencies together with practical information about contacting such agencies. The issue of futures is not handled interactively at this point – participants are usually firmly embedded in a career or are continuing in their education and so their immediate or medium term future is usually unaffected. Some individuals do go through a major transformation concerning future direction. Where this occurs the advice is usually to continue down their current track and take a measured decision about their future over an extended period of time.

B. Debriefing students after field placements

Debriefing students on courses after their time overseas carries a complex set of aims. I often invite students to take the debriefing at three levels. Primarily they need to take it as a time for themselves and their team to close the door on a chapter of their life and be in a place where they can move on. If able they can also view the process of how debriefing is done and think through how they would apply the techniques to their own teams or situations in turn. Thirdly, the courses we run endeavour to use best practice or at least good practice debriefing techniques – students are encouraged to think through debriefing techniques with people in other agencies as and when they move on, based on their own good or bad experience of the methods used below.

From the agencies' perspective and the course leaders perspective there are a number of aims for the time together. Each student needs to have time to feedback what they did, what they accomplished, how they feel about their time away, their return and their future and how their relationship with God has developed, if that is the case. They need to be reminded of any relevant health issues and have a medical examination where necessary. For YWAM (UK) each student is encouraged to leave with a concrete plan of their next career step. Finally each student needs to leave the course, not just physically, but also psychologically and spiritually.

Logistically the planning for such a debriefing is very tight. For most course debriefs the time allocated is five working days with students arriving in sufficient time to be rested (i.e. not significantly jet lagged or exhausted from the outreach itself) and with sufficient space afterwards to catch flights home. Teams are asked to arrive not less than two clear days before the start of the debriefing and to leave not more than three days after the end of debriefing.[5] A sample timetable is outlined in Table 4-2 and is, basically, an expanded version of the Impact Team debriefing schedule. Some additional types of sessions have been put in.

'Personal testimonies' is an opportunity for students to practice giving roughly two – three minutes of testimony or feedback to their church or other groups. Each student is given a maximum of three minutes to feedback to the rest of the school about their experience of the course as a whole. The discipline is, obviously, less of persuading the students to speak but more of helping them to find ways to contain all they have to say to a brief period of time and still be informative. Two classic errors can be made. Students easily fall in to the trap of using jargon or assuming knowledge that the general public may not have. The second trap is the tendency to make grandiose statements about personal spirituality ('God has really improved my preaching skills'). Students are given feedback where appropriate to encourage them to keep the message simple and to

Table 4-2
One week debriefing schedule for students returning from a short term field placement

	8.45	10.00	11.00	11.20	1.00	2.00 – 3.15	7.30
MON.	Worship	Coming Back	Coffee	Personal Testimonies	Lunch	Interviews	Free
TUES.	Free	Team Feedback to group	Coffee	Personal Testimonies	Lunch	Interviews	Team Feedback
WED.	Worship	Team meetings	Coffee	Personal Testimonies	Lunch	Interviews	Team Feedback
THURS	Free	Going home Health reminder	Coffee	Support Raising	Lunch	Interviews	Free
FRI.	Free	Graduation	Coffee	Graduation	Lunch	Interviews	Celebration Meal

avoid talking about their new found abilities, and rather let the fruit of those abilities speak for themselves.

Each student is given a 30 minute interview by an experienced staff member at which current abilities and future career options are examined. Career drift after an often potent experience is not uncommon and students are encouraged to get a grip on implementing what God has been showing them.

The team leaders' meeting is a chance for the team leaders to debrief as a staff group. The purpose is not to give feedback about individual students but rather to debrief their experience of leading.

The aim of graduation is to significantly release each student and staff member from the school and to commission them into their future. By the end of graduation each student and staff member should feel free of the school and each other. It is a time of completion and releasing.

Many different approaches have been used. The one I favour is to gather the whole school community together and then have three or four students 'step forward' when they feel ready. Coming forward is taken to symbolise leaving the school and stepping forward into the future. Each member of the small group is then prayed for individually by the wider school community and then formally released into the future that God has for them by a school leader from the school. The process is repeated until everyone has been prayed for, including the staff.

The dynamic process of the week can be intensely stressful for the school leaders. There can be a tremendous sense of pressure to complete, to finish. Emotions during the week are intense with joyful reunions but quickly followed by the anticipation that the school is about to finish and people split up. Throughout all of that is the sense of accomplishment at completion and of progress which emerges often in the planned worship and the times of spontaneous thanksgiving.

C. *Debriefing programme for Year For God*

The programme outlined in Table 4-3 (Year For God) is designed for teams of people coming home after working a year abroad. They will have experienced the full cycle of cultural orientation, will have made some significant contribution to overseas work yet also will have begun to discover the limitations of short term service in a development context. They are unlikely to fit back easily into their home culture yet will be aware of how limited they actually were overseas. Equally they will have experienced the full cycle of team formation and will have had their share of joys and frustrations with fellow outreach-team members and members of the local permanent team.

The programme contains the same elements as other short term programmes but the programme is stretched over five days with four overnight stays rather than 24 hours with one overnight stay. By the time the debriefing course begins participants will normally have been home for a few weeks.

Table 4-3
Sample 'Year For God' Debriefing

Day 1

11.30	Arrive and coffee
12.30	Lunch
2.00	General introduction to the debrief, outline of the programme
2.15	Hopes of going overseas and fulfilled and unfulfilled expectations
3.15	Tea
3.45	Individual Team Debriefings
5.00	End
6.00	Meal
8.30	Social/video

Day 2

9.30	Team feedback – Each team have half an hour to share about their experiences
10.30	Coffee
11.00	What was it like to leave? Returning to the UK
12.30	Lunch
2.00	The Future
3.00	Tea
3.30	Optional personal interviews
6.00	Meal
8.30	Social/video

Day 3

9.30	Worship & Teaching
11.00	Coffee
11.30	Final session. Was the time valuable?
12.30	Lunch
1.30	Depart

This particular programme begins with lunch. Experience has shown that it is hopeless to try to bring people straight into a meeting, they have far too much to say to one another after a few weeks absence and lunch is usually a lively affair. After lunch staff outline the programme and lay the usual ground rules of confidentiality. Time is then given to exploring the year as a whole and how people experienced it. There are usually several teams present who will have been to quite different continents yet their common experiences quickly begin to show through and a sense of community for the entire group is quickly established.

A sample of responses to the question 'What words would you use to describe the year' is as follows:

tiring, language, fulfilling, stumbling, friendships, grace, amazing, privilege, experience, dependence, gift, marriage, enlightening, frustrating, lonely, stressful, pressure, testing, engrossing, revelatory, dangerous, exciting, stretching, nightmare, challenge, beautiful, learning, people, faithfulness, foundational, laugh, precious, exhilarating, communication.

Each word was carefully chosen and there was an intensity amongst the group as they both listened and heard what was being said. The words carried power and there were frequent nods as people indicated that they knew exactly what was being communicated. Words were positive (grace, amazing, enlightening), negative (frustrating, nightmare, stumbling) and sometimes, just facts of life (tiring).

For many in the group it is the first time they have been able to speak about the year from a position of perspective, i.e. out of the country. It is often the first time they have been able to talk about the year to people who largely understand their comments yet who were not there with them (staff and people from other teams).

A decent break gives participants time to reflect with each other or on their own if they prefer. Following the break the teams are split up and meet with a staff member who either came out to visit the team or with someone who knows the country and the ministry they worked in. As with the short term teams this is a chance for the teams to review their year with one another – by the end of the meeting the aim is for the team to be able to separate from one another and to have resolved any outstanding issues.

The session is scheduled to end well before the evening meal and plenty of time is then available to show photographs to each other, compare notes away from staff and begin to prepare for the informational feedback the following day. The evening has a social feel about it. Many are happy to see a video (nothing too emotive, action packed or 'preachy') or simply hang out with each other. Staff are available but not intrusively so.

The first session the following morning is an opportunity for participants to give a more or less factual account of their time away. It is a chance to talk about what was done and what was accomplished. Again there is a sense that the participants are talking to an informed audience who understand exactly what is being said and are deeply interested in the experiences of others.

After a further coffee break the next session is devoted to 'leaving' and 'returning to the UK'. The replies from one group were as follows in response to 'coming home has been....'

> frustrating, sad, tiring, misunderstanding, strange, confusion, nice-food, cheese, exciting, precious, inactivity, FUTURE??, change, different, weather (boo), mother, fashion, expectations of others, TOILETS (cheers).

The list is notable for its inclusion of good but concrete items (nice food, cheese, toilets). Some people found the return exciting and precious but they also agreed that the overwhelming feelings were those reported first – frustration, tiredness and misunderstanding were universal. Many felt sad not just at leaving the culture and country but also the lifestyle. Teaching input at this point helped to put the feelings in context and to give the participants some degree of insight into the nature, commonality and longevity of their reaction. For many the feelings were in fact at their most intense immediately on return and had abated somewhat by the time they came for debriefing. This is evidenced by replies to another question 'I feel now.....'

> optimistic, cautious, great potential, hopeful, frightened, almost overwhelmed, pastorally responsible, on brink of something new, excited, careful, jigsaw puzzle, directed, privileged, useful, awed, secure in insecurity.

This later list generated after weeks at home is much more complex. It is as if people are coming to terms with being in their historical home, having left a form of home and not really fitting. There is a sense of anticipatory emotion about the future although the question was not directed to the future. The final answer 'secure in insecurity' was not in the least pompous when offered but came as more of an insight into the normal Christian condition.

Time is given to addressing the future although the majority of participants are, in fact, 'gap year' students and so their immediate future is reasonably settled. This session therefore takes time to look at the long term future and the way in which the year has modified or altered future career aspirations or hopes.

Individuals may want to be seen for more extensive career guidance or to talk through individual issues and time is set aside for that. Again there is plenty of time for informal socialising in the evening and the programme may well be hijacked by the participants who want to appreciate the chance to have a final fling together.

The programme the following morning is set aside for giving thanks to God for the year and praying for each individual as they go out. By the end of that session individuals, whether their experience has been good, bad or indifferent, should feel free of the agency and the past year and ready to move on into the future God has for them.

The evaluation session of the debriefing gives staff and participants a chance to feedback on the value of the sessions as a whole. Universally the participants find that the opportunity to be with like-minded people for a short while is invaluable.

D. Long term staff debriefing programme

In considering this course we set four basic aims – that participants would leave the course:

- refreshed
- hopeful
- not isolated
- understanding re-entry

In designing the programme we identified three key components that needed to be present.

(i) Time

We were very aware of the need to run schedules on time. Participants in this kind of course need structure and we felt that a lack of structure would multiply the uncertainty that the people already feel. Along similar lines we debated the value of giving timetable sessions but leaving the content flexible thus being presented as 'session 1', 'session 2' and so on. However it seemed clear that our aim is to reduce uncertainty and ambiguity and, to that end, we decided to be specific in the timetable about what would happen and when.

(ii) Breaks

Much debriefing and private processing occurs over meals or other breaks. The value of having groups of people being debriefed is their shared common experience and their ability to talk informally to one another about that. Whilst staff are available they generally tend not to be going through the re-entry dynamics with the same intensity of the participants. Given that, we run sessions strictly to time and ensure that break times are preserved so that there is plenty of opportunity for informal discussion and private reflection.

(iii) Overnight

Running debriefing seminars to include an overnight stay seems critical. People have the chance to reflect on their experiences overnight and often bring fresh insight or perspective to the process the following morning.

This debriefing is offered to all returning British YWAM staff of whom we are aware. Ideally, potential participants are contacted on their return to the UK and the opportunity to join a debriefing seminar offered to them. The seminar is residential and costs are kept as low as possible. Numbers are kept small (eight or fewer) with two debriefers (one male and one female) attending the entire course.

Programme Details

A sample timetable is in Table 4-4 and the rationale behind each section is laid out below. We have also kept notes from the many sessions that we have undertaken and representative contributions are also outlined below.

Introductions

This time is an opportunity for participants to get to know one another at a factual level, for example where they have been, for how long and the sort of things they have been involved with. Where families are present then all members, including children where at all possible, should be given a voice.

Staff also have opportunity to introduce themselves. Apart from factual information this is also a valuable opportunity for staff to begin establishing their 'credibility' i.e. their ability because of their own past experiences to largely understand what the participants are talking about. Participants will be very aware that no-one can truly understand their situation unless they have 'been there'.

The structure of the course is then explained and some of the ground rules given, in particular that the time is confidential to the group and that people should be free to express whatever they wish during any of the sessions or to others in private.

As part of the introduction participants are often asked to identify their expectations for the weekend. This has a number of purposes. It gives the debriefers some feel of the nature of the group and the type of issues that may come up within sessions. It sets an outline agenda for the group as a whole and gives some ownership to the process and also continues to give everyone in the group a chance to speak.

Typical responses during this time include the need to get to grips with unexpected reverse culture shock, to bring closure to their overseas experience and so to move on, to understand how to cope with the loss associated with their time abroad, to keep hold of the good parts and to bring clarification for the future. Interestingly people are also concerned with the practicalities of life. The changes that have occurred in western life during the last three to ten years are huge and returnees often need help with the activities of daily living.

Hopes on going overseas

This initial session is a straightforward, non-threatening exercise designed to help the participants begin to talk about their experiences in a non-

Table 4-4
Debriefing Course for long term returnees

Friday

2.00 – 4.00	Arrival
4.00 – 5.00	Tea and Introductions – staff – participants – aims and structure of course
5.00 – 5.30	Hopes on going overseas
6.00........	Dinner and free evening (staff available)

Saturday

9.30 – 10.30	Fulfilled and unfulfilled expectations
10.30 – 11.00	Break
11.00 – 12.30	What was it like to leave the field?
1.00............	Lunch
2.30 – 3.30	Coming back to the UK
3.30 – 4.00	Break
4.00 – 5.30	Coming back to the UK
6.00..........	Dinner and free evening (staff available)

Sunday

9.30 – 11.00	Bible study, worship, prayer.
11.00 – 11.30	Break
11.30 – 1.00	The future – where now?
1.00............	Lunch
2.00 – 3.00	Was this time together valuable?
3.00..........	Tea & departure

threatening way and to give them an idea of how the process will work.

Participants often express the common hopes of 'doing a good job', 'seeing people come to Christ' or more inward directed hopes of self-growth. In a humorously self-deprecating way participants will sometimes share their fantasies of being the next Hudson Taylor or Florence Nightingale or their hopes that things could move much faster than they had been taught they would.

The following session on the schedule occurs the next day. Participants have their first meal together along with the staff and there is a chance to relax together.

For the following sessions the timetable has been structured so that sessions do not last longer than 90 minutes primarily for the sake of the participants' stamina. As has been outlined above, sessions run to time so that participants have a predictable breathing space and the safety of a contained amount of time in which to speak or stay silent. Breaks also mean that participants may, if they wish, save their comments for that time for one another, staff or private prayer.

Expectations

For many people the satisfaction or otherwise of their overseas work is less to do with the concrete reality of what they did or experienced and more to do with the match or mismatch between their expectations and what was accomplished.

For a competent community development worker or church planter the first year will be spent in enculturation, language learning and relationship building. If that is the expectation then letters home will be contented, expressing pleasure at the language gains and cultural insights. If the extent of enculturation required is unexpected then the letters home will be full of frustration at the slow pace of life and the lack of accomplishments. The concrete reality is the same, the expectations quite different.

To that end a conversation about expectations towards the beginning of the debriefing time is helpful. Participants have the energy to think about dynamics which may not be immediately pressing. The dynamics which may be of immediate concern can wait a while until a context has been given.

When reflecting on unfulfilled expectations participants often concentrate on practical issues:

relationship with the local community, becoming fluent in the language, help with housing, pastoral care and, generally, feeling unsupported.

By contrast fulfilled expectations can be more tangential:

simpler lifestyle, bringing children up innocently and so on.

A profound insight from one participant was the notion of fulfilled expectations which were taken for granted – for example coming back healthy or, indeed, coming back alive.

There may also be time to talk about the unexpected – issues which were not expectations but which simply had not occurred to participants. These have included issues such as taking on significant responsibility on arrival, the insularity of the expatriate community and the totally different way of thinking (not just language) of the nationals.

Dealing with the issue of expectations often leads to insights on the extent to which participants, despite training to the contrary, had actually held on to hopes for a Western lifestyle, grateful nationals and powerful personal ministry. Project based workers in particular had usually gone out with the expectation (rather than hope) that the project would be successful in terms of outcome measures.

Very often there is an opportunity for one of the staff to give a very simple outline of a relevant theory of culture, cultural adjustment or team natural history. Participants don't need an extended teaching, they are well able to fill in the gaps for themselves. The power often comes in the insights they gain as their experiences are validated and their thinking crystallised by the teaching process. The most powerful insight seems to come from Kwast's[6] concentric circle model as participants draw out the implications for themselves. (See Chapter 3).

There are a range of other questions which may be asked and such questions will depend very much on the nature of the group being debriefed. Sample questions include how participants would have done things differently and things they wished they had known.

Leaving the field

The issue of leaving is typically one of the most difficult issues long term staff face. Guilt may be present because of work left incomplete or friends left behind in difficult circumstances. There may be pleasure at a job well done yet accompanying anxiety about the future of the work or ministry and the people involved. Coupled with that are the inevitable stresses and strains of packing a home and finding somewhere new to live. Set out in Table 4-5 are some of the comments people have made about leaving.

For many the memory of leaving is one of intense mixed emotions. Participants report the sense of pleasure at the thought of returning and yet the intensity of their existence overseas is difficult to surrender. Deep friendships have often been made and the pain of leaving them, possibly never to see them again, is often acute. There is often considerable joy at the accomplishments of the time away coupled with frustration that more could not have been done.

The dynamic of departure seems to bring into sharp focus the hopes and expectations that participants had on their arrival and the extent to which those have been fulfilled or not. For some participants departure also brings insight into perceptions of their own adequacy or perceived inadequacy.

Marjory Foyle's insight into the grieving nature of entry finds its reprise at this point of re-entry but more obviously. For the debriefer the task at this point is often to enable the participants to grieve or at least give them permission to grieve. Sometimes the process has been blocked by no

> **Table 4-5**
> **Comments made about leaving**
>
> *Relief* to be leaving the dynamics of particular community, at leaving a tough situation, at leaving the fishbowl of Christian community.
>
> *Mixed emotions/turmoil*: glad/sad to leave, confusion about leaving – why, where now, God's sense of call yet guilt at leaving; coping with the nationals asking why we were leaving.
>
> *Mourning process*: so much to do and loss of opportunity to complete the task, sense of leaving home, sadness of leaving friends, sense of overall loss.
>
> *Change*: biggest change; anticipating extreme change; apprehensive at consequences of letting go.
>
> *Positive*: much easier to leave, to sell up and to process the decision than expected. Sense of completion, of time to move on, sense of belonging to the culture and so not losing everything as I moved on.

more than inadequate time or lack of a safe place to do the grieving. Unless one uses a particularly inexpensive airline it is difficult to take more than 24 hours to move from leaving grieving friends and one's entire life to greeting family and friends who are thrilled at your return and seem to want to hear all about it. One arrives 'home' not only jet lagged but also emotion lagged.

Ninety minutes to cover such issues can seem laughably short. How on earth can one process the depth of emotion apparently represented by this session? The answer is simply that one can't and shouldn't even try. In working with returning missionaries one is, by and large, working with very intact, whole people who need little more than the reassurance that what they are feeling is valid and normal and for those feelings and dynamics to be identified. The remainder of the process will follow naturally and can be done in private or with friends. It does not need the ministrations of counsellors, therapists or other 'professionals' to be completed. Often towards the end of a session the room can become still with the intensity of the emotion. The temptation for the debriefers is to try to make it all right, to offer prayers of peace or to offer ministry. This is the worst thing to offer people who are going through a normal, if painful process. They don't want peace, just at that moment. They are not in need of healing. To do so would be to deny the reality of the friends and ministry they have left and which they miss so terribly. They want to go and have a good cry, or yell, by themselves, with God or, very occasionally, with another. They want to grieve and should be given the status and dignity accorded to all grieving people – space to get on with it.

At the end of this session it is not at all uncommon to see a few people apparently flee. They are not running away from the pain, they are running into it. The debriefers need to get out of the way and not chase after them to see if they are OK. Of course they are not – but that is fine. If they want help they'll come and ask. Usually they don't and usually they are back, ready to go, at the start of the subsequent session.

Part of the thinking behind this comes from a very high view that the author holds of the priesthood of all believers. Christ is our great high priest not another person. Yet sometimes, in our eagerness to help others, we get between them and Christ – we become, in the wrong sense, that person's priest. I have many memories of my introductory course with YWAM. One of the most startling is of a very anointed speaker coming to teach on some subject or other. The content matters less now than how he handled the 'ministry time' afterwards. Instead of asking if people would like to come forward for prayer he simply prayed out loud for a short while asking God to bless the class. On completion he quietly left, leaving the class praying on their own about the things they had learnt.

The lesson came home powerfully to me – sometimes people can come to us for help rather than going to God themselves. There are occasions where we need 'flesh and blood' but the counsellor's boundary is clear in never taking the place of Christ in that person's life.

Mercifully, at this stage in the proceedings, comes lunch which means that most people have more than adequate time and space to reflect on the morning session.

After lunch we take the two sessions in the afternoon to talk about coming home.

Coming Home

For most participants who have been home for more than a few weeks the pleasures of western society and the attention of friends and family has worn thin. The sense of isolation is acute and few solutions have been generated to help. The time away is too close to have been fully resolved and the sense of quiet, polite, desperation is evident.

The topic needs little introduction – asking what words people would use to describe coming home usually induces a few hollow laughs followed by what feels like a torrent of pent up emotion. Even quieter participants perk up and offer some thoughts. Keeping on top of it can be a struggle. (Table 4-6). The debriefer can sometimes feel abused in the ambiguity of the participants uncertainty of quite who to blame for their

> **Table 4-6**
> **Sample comments about coming home for long term staff:**
>
> Climate – feeling the cold
> Food – can't find things used to
>   – expensive/unhealthy/waste
>   – enjoying home food
> Choice in shops/ obscenity/ materialism
> Guilt at being here
> Waste of resources
> Temptation to judge
> Struggle with people complaining about trivialities
> The news is simply entertainment
> No friends
> Being surrounded by non Christians
> Having money
> Clothes – different here
> Pressure to make decisions – results oriented society
> No one to bounce thoughts off
> Church orientation in ministry
> Whose spiritual authority are we under
> Practicalities of re-entry
> People don't understand the idea of sabbatical
> Island mentality
> Unknown terminology
> New words, forgotten words
> Political correctness
> EEC issues
> Leaner/meaner Britain
> Lack of tolerance
> Greetings – how to do them
> Lack of spontaneous hospitality

sometimes unholy thoughts. Eventually the thought will occur that no one has really empathised with group members in what they have been experiencing and the group relaxes as they find one another in, to use Nouwen *et al's* phrase,[7] their common vulnerability. The temptation is for the debriefer to comment. That is usually superfluous – the participants understand, finally, and have one another for a moment. The debriefer becomes redundant and healing begins to occur where we should always expect it to – in the body of the group.

At this point it may be helpful to begin to draw out both the common

Table 4-7
Practical information returning UK YWAM long term missionaries identified as needing prior to arrival or on arrival after an absence of eight years or more

Financial:

Entitlement to State income

Income support
Housing benefit
Council tax benefit/registration
Child benefit
No education grant if out of country for more than three years prior to start of course

Outgoings

Maternity allowance as function of NI contributions
Credit cards/debit cards/bank accounts/switch cards
Existence of cash back at supermarkets
Benefits of renting vs purchasing house
Pension/private health schemes/life insurance
Tax liability & responsibility

The basics

Currency – the coins & notes. Typical prices
Phone cards – what are they & where to buy
No more buying tickets on trains
Typical budget for living in UK
Schools – the difference between grant maintained, State etc.

Medical
Medical card
GP/dentist/optician – registering/ non NHS etc.
Cars – insurance + non contributory bonus proof
Using the Citizens Advice Bureau

Car and home
MOT
Tax Disc
TV licence

Current affairs
Digest of recent UK news

themes from the white-board as well as the common issues that are present in re-entry. For many participants they have been baffled by the frustration they feel with loved ones. They have been hurt by the apparent lack of interest shown by others in their recent history. The sense of isolation is clear.

Going through the fairly complex reactions which surround the issue of guilt and sense of injustice is also helpful. Many will have had their 'supermarket' experience or something akin to it. Outlining the competitive nature of western conversation frequently produces insight into recent conversations that have gone wrong.

However, for most people, the healing has begun as they gain hope that they are not, actually, alone in the process they are experiencing, that it is normal and has a natural course to run. In all of this the aim is not to 'make it better' but rather to account for the feelings people have and thus give them perspective, hope and a degree of control. As is emphasised continually, we are not dealing with a clinical population of neurotic adults, we are dealing with a selected group of competent adults who are going through an entirely reasonable set of responses to loss and to identity struggles.

A further helpful dynamic has been the gathering of the kind of information that people feel they need to know when they return home. They are the things that people take for granted and never think to tell them. This is outlined in Table 4-7.

Futures
Table 4-8 outlines a set of responses from one group concerning the future. By and large the group is hopeful but there is an underlying feeling of a very open future with too many opportunities and options[8]. God is good and in charge. This particular session is often the most difficult to contain since, at the time of the debriefing, participants will have often been unable to devote much energy to the issue. It is however a major concern for participants who often feel they have 'missed the boat' and either feel they have made themselves unemployable or who have such strong feelings of not fitting that they may have little motivation to think about a future 'back home'. This session is more about expressing thoughts, hopes and fears of the future and, in that, finding support from those around. The time cannot be an individual 'career guidance' session but rather devoted towards helping participants, as necessary, to summon up the will to seek God for the future He desires for them.

Going home
Coming back 'home' can be a very difficult transition. Those who have stayed behind may not have changed as much but things will *seem* very different to returnees because of the changes they have experienced in themselves as they lived abroad.

Table 4-8
Sample group comments about personal future

So many opportunities – but like broken jigsaw
Open doors – wish God would close some
So *many* factors
Opportunities for re-firing – broaden, opportunities
Nappies – encore!!
200m course (hurdles, uphill, mist)
Excitement – something new vs anxiety/panic we'll never know, never do anything again
Reassurance/hopeful/positive outlook
Confidence in God
Family considerations

There will also be the expectation that people will be interested, if not fascinated, by the returnee's exploits, particularly family and close friends. It is helpful to pause at some stage prior to returning home and ask how realistic that is. If the returnee's family never showed much of an interest in their old, secular, job why should things be different now? If their family took a keen interest in all that they did there is every reason for that to continue. Amongst friends the same dynamic applies. If the extent of the relationship with the returnee's 'best friend' was someone they played squash with every Friday night why should they suddenly become interested in what the returnee has been doing? Alternatively if best friends were people with whom the returnee tended to share their life then that has every likelihood of continuing. Another helpful question to ask is who the returnee heard from whilst overseas. Not – who did they receive form newsletters from or who promised to write but could never get round to it but who actually wrote. A way of considering this in reverse is to think about newsletters home. For some people a scribbled name at the bottom is enough, for others a brief 'ps', for yet others an extensive 'ps'. For a very few, maybe one or two, letters or e-mails were composed as opposed to sending out newsletters. In all probability those who received letters and the few who received extensive notes on the newsletters will be those who it is easier to communicate with on returning.

The reasons why people find it hard to listen has been outlined in Chapter 3 (competitive conversation, inability to relate and guilt). There are a series of strategies which can be used though to increase the probability of being heard.

A key issue is to be satisfactorily debriefed, i.e. to get the intensity of the time away out of the debriefee's system. Friends and family are not debriefers – they want the story version of what it was like to be away coupled with some thoughts and feelings. What is difficult to handle is raw emotion connected with extreme events. The joy of being caught up in seeing a church planted or seeing a healthcare project established can be intense. Equally the pain of helplessly watching someone die of an entirely preventable disease in the midst of poverty and injustice is difficult to report without the listener feeling as if they are being berated for not doing something about the situation. Returnees' feelings are often intense and need to die down a bit before people generally feel able to handle listening to the stories.

The list of potential people to talk to both in the early stages and later is actually quite long. The obvious people who are best able to understand are colleagues and team mates. The probable reason for the 'success' of 'veterans' associations such as the British Legion is the very fact that it brings together people who have shared things which are really quite difficult to speak about. Veterans associations bring together people who have a common vulnerability. The battles of yesterday can be spoken about but only satisfactorily to those who fully understand the words, those who were there.

Aspects of overseas work can be talked through in astonishing detail with people who are considerably older. I was once talking to a group of seventy year olds about some work I had been doing abroad. I described getting water from a well. The group came to life and wanted details of the water, the way the water was drawn, where the well was sited. They then went on to describe, for the benefit of me, the youngster, the comparative advantages of wells in the villages nearby during their youth.

Former missionaries are an invaluable source of informed discussion on overseas service. Some care needs to be taken here however. Modern missions is quite different to classic missions. The length of service was very different and there may be a point of contention between the modern missionary who has been overseas for 'only' five years and the classic missionary who was just getting into their stride at that point. Work practices have changed – church planting classically was establishing a denomination – the modern penchant for indigenous churches may cause a raised eyebrow. Medical missions, classically, was about missionary hospitals. To some ex-missionaries the modern aim of primary health care cannot possibly be a serious use of time. However, with appropriate care, details of the outreach can be shared to considerable mutual benefit. A colleague of mine was to visit Mozambique on one occasion and spoke about her forthcoming trip to some local retired missionaries. They were very excited and asked her to bring back any news she could of the area they had worked in for many years.

Other aid workers can also be a good source of mutual support. Again some care needs to be taken. It seems an unfortunate fact of life that there exists considerable competition between agencies and the conversation can quickly degenerate into the worst form of competitive conversation of the 'my life was harder than yours' variety.

Missionaries' return to their home church is a minefield of contrasting expectations, hopes and misperceptions. Consider one returning missionary's first Sunday morning back at her home church. She notes the absence of a ticker tape welcome for the returning hero and has never seen the steward on the door before in her life. 'Welcome', he says, 'are you visiting'?

There are a number of options at this point. The most mature is probably to continue on in through the door and find a friendly face. This is not the time to think what to say, it is best to have already given that some thought and also adjusted expectations. The missionary is not so important that the whole church stops for her. This moment is a defining one for her – it shows where her treasure is. To paraphrase Christ – 'I tell you truly, those who boast of their exploits in my service have their reward already'. Is our treasure in the admiration of others for our deeds or is it in the quiet knowledge that our treasure is in heaven where moth and rust cannot eat it away?

Our attitude should be the same as that of Christ Jesus.... He came to serve. As the missionary walks to the person she feels able to talk to, she isn't asking ask how she can get her story out in the best way, but rather asking how she can serve them. Some people will need to tell of their recent past. Others will be truly delighted to see an old friend and will want to hear all there is to say. Still others will feel that only the missionary should speak since what they have to say is unimportant.

Invariably people in the home church will need help with the details of the conversation. The answer to the question 'how are you' is not 'fine' with the hope they will then move on to ask the appropriate probing questions but rather something which gives them a stepping stone into the conversation. Giving some concrete information such as 'fine, I've just got back from Malawi' will help to provide such a link. Most people will go on to ask for some sort of clarification – at that point it is helpful to have some sort of brief story to tell. And that usually will do. The missionary is there to serve – if friends want more information they'll ask for it. However they have shown an interest in the missionary's life – now it is their turn to give information. How are they? What is going on in their life? What has been happening in the church and so on.

Feeding back to a formal church presentation is quite different. Here there may be ample opportunity to present for an entire service or for an entire evening meeting. Alternatively the minister may ask for the entire overseas experience to be encapsulated in a two minute presentation during a service. Whatever the request it should be honoured. In the parable of the talents Jesus reminds us that those who are entrusted with little and who honour that trust will then be trusted with much. As the church sees the honouring of the little things so the probability is that the returnee will be entrusted with more. It's that servant heart again.

During presentations it is helpful to paint word pictures and tell stories. We have all been subjected to enough tedious missionary presentations without adding to the catalogue. People do not want to hear a blow by blow account of overseas travel, they need a synopsis of significant activities to get a flavour of what happened. Such presentations can be key in someone else being called to the field. Research by Kimber[9] suggests that the most significant factor influencing people to go on to the mission field was a missionary speaker presentation.

Using slides is a particular skill. All too often people use them as the script – 'this is a picture of me at the airport, and now one of me on the plane' and so on. It is better by far to use the pictures to illustrate what is being said – to enhance the story, not tell it.

Official church groups will also need to have their reports and feedback. It is wise to give such reports even if they are not asked for and particularly if the church has been financially supportive in any way. Particular groups, such as the missions board or the eldership of the church may need a factual synopsis of what was planned, what was accomplished and what has changed as a result.

Worship and bible study

The next session for participants is a time of worship, bible study and intercession. There has been considerable discussion about the form of this as the courses have developed over the last few years. Several principles were clear. The service had to be uniquely meaningful to the participants and conducted in such a way that they were able to draw closer to God and also glorify Him.

In thinking about the worship it therefore seemed appropriate perhaps to have a time of singing but also to have a time of reflection with participants bringing their own material, perhaps a poem, bible passage, flower or something which, to them, represented what they were trying to say to or about God.

For us the bible study had to be 'meaty' – something the participants could get their teeth into and be fed by. We were conscious that, for many, they had been the ones giving out for so long and had now returned home to possibly good but often irrelevant teaching.

Intercession was perhaps the biggest risk. Words for many would not do. For us we needed some simple way of bringing our prayers to God without denigrating the power of what was being communicated with mere words. To the majority of the Christian world the solution we adopted will seem hauntingly familiar. The church down the centuries has lit candles as part of intercession – or lit a candle to represent *Lumen Christi* – the light of Christ, *Lumen Mundi* – the light of the world.

One woman lit her candle to represent the work of Christ amongst the millions of street children in Brazil. On that sunny Sunday morning none of us could look at that candle without feeling something of the passion of Christ for those children. Few of us could have been as eloquent with our words as that candle was once lit.

The 'service' takes as long as is right. It is often a time of quietness, meditation, peace, hope. A quiet understanding that our aloneness is false – Christ has walked where we walked and Christ goes ahead of us to show us the way.

After lunch there is opportunity for the participants to feed back to the staff their perceptions of the time together. The following is an amalgam of the feedback received over some five courses and two years.

COURSE STRUCTURE

- Good to have time out/away from work/ rest in God over an entire weekend and to take time to think about debriefing issues.
- The way in which the course was structured (order, sessions running to time and not too long) was helpful.
- Questions – writing things down (good) – perhaps give questions the day before.
- The size of the group had been just right to process the information, to pray effectively and also to pray in detail.
- Good to be around people who *understand* therefore feel less alone.

COURSE DYNAMIC

- YWAM making the effort helps me feel more valued.
- To acknowledge that mission is not always easy helps.
- Helpful to look backwards and forwards with people who are also at the same stage.
- Re-entry is very similar to bereavement process and so need people to be there.
- The situations I faced were put in front of me and I was able to talk about the negative side of things without being criticised.
- Non pressured and relaxed.
- The staff had been able to identify with participants.
- There was a good balance between informal sessions and teaching.
- There were practical ideas for coping with re-entry shock.
- There were practical ideas for relating back home to church and family.
- Conflict resolution was handled well.

COURSE OUTCOME

- It helped me to realise that I *do* still care for the people out there.

- I came very stuck and heavy hearted but am now able to look back at the good things that happened.
- Helped to focus on fulfilled things.
- Gained insights into why I was feeling the way I was.
- Very reassured that what we were experiencing was normal.

The structure of the course seems particularly suited to long term staff returning from overseas. Time away from the day-to-day life to give a proper time of reflection to an important aspect of one's life is not, it seems, an idle luxury, but rather something which is essential. The structure given to the weekend as a whole has been universally appreciated. People have generally had their fill of uncertainty and find the structure and discipline of the weekend containing and releasing.

The chance to say whatever they wished without fear of rebuke or repercussion was immensely freeing for participants. The pressures, as many have said, of having lived in a 'Christian goldfish bowl' are immense. Many returnees are leaders and so the pressures experienced on the field were multiplied since they often had few or no peers to relate to.

Participants are helped by the balance between the debriefers hearing what is being said, teaching about the dynamics being represented, and giving practical ideas for coping with returning.

The outcomes are clear. By and large people coming to the course come with some uncertainty as to their experiences and why they are feeling as they do. Most are isolated and feeling the need to be less alone. The course gives participants insight into their situation, empowers them through those insights and then frees them up to move on into a new place with God and in His service.

5. DEBRIEFING INDIVIDUALS OR COUPLES

There are comparative advantages and disadvantages to briefing individuals as opposed to debriefing groups. There needs to be considerable clarity of thinking through the reasons for individual debriefing. There is no evidence to support the idea that individual debriefing has any advantage over debriefing people in groups. Normally individual routine debriefing will be done for logistical reasons. The commonest reasons would be agencies which receive back only a few people per year, insufficient to form a group within three months of return and where a decision has been taken in principle to debrief in-house rather than use an external agency.

Other reasons for individual debriefing may be the return of seasoned staff, well used to re-entry, who have specific issues they wish to be debriefed about and an individual's specific request to be seen individually.

Where individual routine debriefings are chosen as the way forward the comparative time investment can be very heavy. If an agency, for example, receives ten people back per year and sees them individually for 3 hours then the total time invested is 30 hours. The same people could be seen in a group and the total agency time for the same outcome is twelve hours using one of the programmes above. This solution may be impractical for some agencies since some people might have to wait up to a year to be seen. It might be possible in this scenario to arrange to see people every six months and the total agency time is six hours as opposed to thirty. Other agencies offer one off fifty minute sessions or one off three hour sessions.

The standard we have set for individual debriefing is to set aside two working days per client and to see the client for alternate hours throughout the two days. Three areas are explored. The first is the concrete nature of what the client did, (for many agencies they will also have prepared a written report for their own managers). The second is their thoughts and feelings about leaving, returning home and being at home. The third area are their hopes for the future.

The individual debriefing session can, in some ways, become quite intense and it is important to prevent the dynamic from straying too far onto a counselling session. Again, the clients need reassuring that what they are be experiencing is normal and to be expected. The aim of the sessions is to leave the client feeling empowered and hopeful for the future.

A very helpful use of individual debriefing is the focused debriefing, almost ventilation, of an individual making repeated short term tours overseas and where the time between each visit is brief. Relief workers and project managers particularly fall into this category and they are often unwilling or unable to participate in a full scale debriefing weekend each time they return home. For such workers a full debriefing may also be inappropriate since they do not perceive themselves as returning home permanently but rather as simply home on leave.

For these workers time with an individual debriefer who knows them well and, hopefully, is available to see them each time they return is invaluable. The agenda for such a meeting is different again. The topic needs to be contained to allowing the client to put their feelings and thoughts into perspective. For many clients it is enough that another person is listening and, through that, validating their experiences. Generally the debriefing will focus less on what was done (again written reports will have been expected by the majority of agencies) and more on helping the client to process their recent thoughts and actions with a non judgmental, but credible, debriefer.

6. DEBRIEFING CHILDREN[10]

Marjory Foyle[11] reminds us that children overseas are often considerably more exposed to the culture than their parents. They are usually better at the local language and more integrated into society via the schooling and friendships they make. Consequently the adjustment to entering their native country can be more intense than that of their parents.

A critical difference is that children, either in reality or in their perception, may not be travelling home but may well be travelling to a foreign country which is not at all home.

The debriefing of children of missionaries is therefore quite different to that of their parents. Children have quite different ways of perceiving to those of adults. They may well be experiencing entry adjustment not re-entry adjustment. They may have had input into the decision to return but they were not in control of the final decision. They may well be feeling the change even more passionately than their parents.

One very fluent 14 year old girl summed it up with the description of her first day at school in England. She described the initial conversation with classmates of outlining that she had just come from Kenya. 'Is that in the east of England'? was the serious response from one peer. On entering the class she sat stunned as the children noisily ignored the teacher's entrance and seemed to have no desire to get on with work. Break time was worse – the conversation centred on minuscule fashion details and pop groups she had never heard of. Yet, as she put it, the previous month she had had to cope with corrupt police, street poverty, dealing in two languages and cultures, doing homework and having a wary eye on national and international politics because it mattered – '....yet all my classmates can think of is the length of their flipping skirts' was her heart-felt summary. Going to see the film Lion King provided light relief – the animals had Swahili names even if the pronounciation was awful.

At this point a melancholy fifteen year old member of the group stirred himself – 'yeah, and last month I was drumming for the local church and speaking Spanish all the time – that was cool. My friends here now, they don't know nothing about nothing'.

Debriefing children has many of the same characteristics as for adults. Sessions need to be bounded by time and topic. Complete confidentiality is needed, including from parents, unless something very serious emerges which parents have to be aware of. The debriefer needs to be on the children's wavelength, ideally a former child of a missionary themselves (credibility factor – although simply being an adult can often provide sufficient credibility for all but the most cynical teenager).

The techniques however vary in detail. Session times will have to be considerably shorter and, for younger children, can only realistically last half a day at a time.

For most children, including teenagers up to about 16, talking on its own is simply unrealistic. Other equipment has to be present to help them walk through their experiences. Maps, large sheets of paper, pens, dolls (male, female, child, baby), Lego etc. are all extremely helpful. Experienced children's workers will be well aware that the floor is vastly preferable to working on a table.

The best resource for those about ten and up is simply a large sheet of paper and a rerun of the white board approach but with the children writing their own words on the sheet and then discussing their contributions afterwards. Obviously this is all best done on the floor or round a table with a 'graffiti' approach which is not too formal. Other more creative ways can also be used, for example a timeline or time-path drawn on individual sheets with the children then drawing or writing significant events onto the sheet, again for discussion afterwards.

For one particular group this approach was so successful that the facilitator became redundant – the teenagers involved emerged from their lunch break and simply asked if they could carry on, all the facilitator needed to do was provide the questions – they'd catch up at break time with any feedback, which they duly did.

For teenagers or those approaching their teens the feedback from this approach is remarkably similar to adults. They feel less isolated, more understood and grateful for the chance to talk about how they feel to someone who understands. They are also grateful for the insights they receive along the way, particularly the confirmation that they are quite entitled to their feelings when someone asks them for the nth time if they are happy to be 'home' – "when will they realise 'home' is two thousand miles away and I miss it badly"?

For younger children it is difficult to assess how critical debriefing is. Developmentally they are considerably more likely to accept that home is where their parents are and, usually, younger children are adept at making new friendships. There is a transitory sense of loss of significant others (pets, friends, surroundings). However it seems that, providing the parents are secure, the move will produce little lasting harm anymore than a move from one town to another within the UK would be harmful in the long run.

7. OUTCOME STUDIES

At the time of writing there are no outcome studies known to me of the validity, success or otherwise of routine debriefing programmes nor are any in preparation. Workers are therefore reliant on participants' self report and the 'compliance' of participants with debriefing programmes as a gauge of the face validity of such programmes. The studies required are complex to establish, requiring some dozens of participants in several matched groups – a control group who do not go on overseas placement; an overseas group who are debriefed on their return and an overseas group who are not debriefed on their return. Such a study, whilst theoretically possible, has already to my knowledge been submitted for ethical approval and refused.

The other option is a longitudinal study of a cohort to establish patterns of mental health morbidity at various points in individual's lives. Again no such study is underway.

We are therefore left with participants' self report which is unequivocally favourable at the time of the debriefing seminar. Of several hundred participants surveyed by questionnaire at the end of debriefing seminars over several years none have found the experience unhelpful and most have found it helpful in the sense of 'reassuring'.

However the attendance at debriefing seminars is not universal and it may be that those who do not attend are a self selected group who would find the experience unhelpful. It is also entirely unproven at the moment that the complex programs described above are necessary. An agreed date, a venue and plenty of refreshments may be all that is required under the guise of 'Reunion'. The argument against this is again the self report of participants claiming to have received valuable insights from the process beyond simply the experience of 'coffee with like minded, similarly experienced people'.

Certainly the programmes described here appear to be doing their job in the sense that, of the seven hundred routinely debriefed over the last eight years none are known to have gone on to experience significant mental health problems as result of their experiences beyond the transitory grief reactions that might be anticipated. Equally the group is highly selected, young, motivated and, by and large, well educated. It is therefore entirely possible that one would expect the prevalence of mental health problems in such a group to be approaching zero.

Research is needed into the effects of debriefing, the necessary components of such programmes and the structure of such programmes. As will be seen in Chapter 6 the same criticism may be made of the debriefing of those experiencing trauma and, for the time being, one must assume that the priority for research funding will be in that direction.

[1] The 'overseas missions manual' is an internal attempt by YWAM (UK) to document its procedures with respect to those sent abroad by YWAM (UK).
[2] Research by Debbie Lovell reported in an unpublished internal YWAM document concerning short term team members during the summer of 1998.
[3] See Chapter 6 for a further discussion on the personal characteristics required of debriefers.
[4] Non attenders fall into two groups, those with important prior commitments such as a family wedding and those who would find it difficult to attend because of perceived failure or feelings of antagonism. Every effort is made to encourage the latter to attend but, inevitably, a very few refuse.
[5] In practice most teams arrive about three days in advance and the majority of students leave within 24 hours of the final event of the debriefing.
[6] ibid.
[7] Nouwen et al, ibid.
[8] Those with a psychoanalytic approach may want to consider just why it is that so many returnees find retail choice so deeply difficult – the thought occurs that it resonates deeply with the range of life choices suddenly open to the returnee.
[9] Sandra Kimber, *Let Me Go*, Evangelical Missionary Alliance, London, 1994.
[10] O'Donnell and O'Donnell 1988 op cit. have a section of their book devoted to some of the wider issues involved in supporting Missionary Kids. The published abstracts of Euro-Comet 1992, a conference on the support of children of missionaries is also very helpful in considering issues beyond the scope of this book.
[11] Foyle 1987 op cit.

Chapter 5

Training the Debriefers

In-house training for those involved in debriefing has been established for several years within YWAM (UK). Training courses have been held in England, Scotland and France. Four groups of people have been identified as requiring training – personnel staff, leaders of schools, desk officers and others directly involved with staff on the field or those explicitly involved with general debriefing. Other writers have identified training needs for people explicitly identified as 'member care workers'.[1] It is my contention that it is best to equip those who have routine contact with missionaries and aid workers rather than setting up a separate type of support group to add to existing support structures.

In planning these courses a distinction has been made between teaching participants about debriefing and skilling participants to *do* debriefing. By and large the essence of debriefing can be put across to a large audience in a few hours. However the audience will not, in any sense, be empowered or become skilled at the practice of debriefing. Training courses, of necessity need to be either staff intensive and of moderate size or, simply, small. To date both types have been run. For the quality of output the preferable size is six or seven participants with one, preferably two, experienced facilitators.

The content of the course and the rough timings are laid out in Table 5-1. The course has been run six times with some 50 participants in total[2] both from YWAM and other agencies. In devising this form of training we have realised that there are several considerations to be borne in mind.

Participants, by and large, are not psychologically trained nor do they necessarily have a training in counselling or personnel management. They are, however, highly motivated to help those for whom they are institutionally responsible. Their previous experience of debriefing others is often haphazard and many report feelings of powerlessness when faced with the issues people talk about on their return. The course was therefore established both to give participants the skills they needed as debriefers and also to empower them, i.e. build their confidence.

Time is precious in the middle management structures of aid agencies and missionary agencies. It is difficult for people to get away from their responsibilities as there are few people to delegate that responsibility to. The course therefore had to be long enough to equip people for the task but brief enough to facilitate attendance. Two days seemed to be the optimum for this and the course therefore had to be accommodated within that

Table 5-1
Training Course for Routine Debriefing
Handout to participants

The aim of the course is to train those attending in how to debrief people returning routinely from service overseas. Particular focus will be given to short term teams but attention will also be given to some long term scenarios. After the first hour or so of introductions the course will be highly interactive and practical.

Day 1

- 10.00 Meet together
- 10.05 Why are you here!?
- 10.15 Six components of briefing
- 10.35 Five different types of clients presenting for debriefing
- 10.45 Six common issues people bring for debriefing
- 11.00 Coffee
- 11.20 Six common issues people bring for debriefing (contd)
- 11.40 Three dynamics in debriefing
- 12.00 Introduction to debriefing exercises
- 12.15 Simulation
- 12.45 Lunch break
- 2.00 Review morning sessions
- 2.15 Simulations
- (3.00 – 3.15 Tea break)
- 4.00 Review of day
- 4.15 Finish

Day 2

- 10.00 Meet together with those overnight questions
- 10.15 Simulations
- 11.00 Coffee

either:
- 11.15 – 12.15 Simulations or: Putting your own debriefing programme together
  - 11.15 Introduction
  - 11.30 Group work
  - 12.00 Feedback
- 12.45 Lunch
- 2.00 Review
- 2.15 This is all very well but what if things go badly wrong?
- 2.45 Conflict
- 3.15 Death and serious injury on the field
- 3.45 Review – debriefing of the course
- 4.15 Finish

time frame. We also decided to equip people solely for routine debriefing (which is by far the norm anyway) which involves teaching the basics of listening skills and the dynamics returnees typically experience. The emphasis was to be on skill transfer and, whilst difficult to reconcile, there was therefore a minimum of theoretical input and a maximum of application.

The programme both modelled and taught good practice in the area. Sessions ran to time and with clear boundaries for breaks. The emphasis was on team debriefings since that is the major debriefing that is done but scope was also available to discuss and practice individual debriefing situations as well. Debriefing was portrayed as standard practice, not an optional extra and particular reference was increasingly made to the implications of the Macnair report and the subsequent People In Aid Code of Best Practice.[3] Debriefing was also portrayed as a standard activity which is not the necessary province of experts but rather well within the ability of most people involved in any pastoral way with missionaries. The need for clinical intervention was kept to the rare circumstances surrounding Post Traumatic Stress Disorder or other presenting serious psychiatric problems.

The first session gives opportunity for people to experience working together in a group and see how that is contained and structured by the facilitators of the course. Two questions have been asked during the first session viz. – 'why do debriefing?' and 'why are you here'? The first question gives a working baseline for the knowledge participants have at the beginning of the course and enables the participants and the facilitators to check what has been learnt by the end of the course. The second question gives the facilitators a chance to understand the motivations of those attending the course and to construct a set of objectives to be checked during the course and at its completion.

People's perceptions of the value of debriefing at the beginning of the course have tended to fall into three categories. A full list of typical responses is given in Table 5-2 (next page).

Institutional reasons are cited. For example there is the desire to improve training by talking to people at the end of their experiences, to protect the agency's reputation and wanting people to stay in missions. Secondly, debriefing is perceived as of inherent benefit to returning staff and students – e.g. preventing feelings of failure, resolving positive and negative emotions and bringing closure, particularly to teams. Finally people believe there is an inherent obligation to provide something for those who are returning – it demonstrates that we care about them as people.

Those attending the course reported wanting to help others adjust to returning home by becoming more skilled. The majority of people attending have been actively involved in debriefing others and have, themselves, worked overseas.

Table 5-2
Response from course participants – why do debriefing?

(italics added at end of course)

- want people to stay in missions – including children of missionaries
- to see that what has happened has been real (*what was real, what did happen?*)
- prevent/expose feelings of failure
- part of re-entry process (being prepared)
- affirm the good in what has happened
- affirm what God has done (*acknowledged where you feel God has 'failed'*)
- memorial stones
- forum for expression
- give feeling of completion (*resolution of conflict*) (*bring conflict into the open*)
- focus/verbalise
- may not otherwise say it
- express things objectively
- get in touch – can come back later if not resolved
- unload +ve & -ve – otherwise remains inside
- even the +ve can be a problem
- equip by learning from experience
- bring closure – especially to group that won't be together again

The following sections of the course are given over to teaching didactically the components of briefing, the types of clients presenting for debriefing, the issues people tend to bring for debriefing and an outline of the methods used in debriefing. All of these have been elaborated in Chapter 4.

Following the presentation the participants embark on an extensive use of simulations (Appendix 1). The focus of the course is skill transfer and this is best achieved through role plays which are monitored and critiqued. Each role play or simulation is an outline of a typical re entry scenario. No major problems are simulated which would distract participants' attention from the key issues that people routinely face in missionary or aid work. Each role play can be presented in a team scenario or as an individual scenario. Course participants take it in turns to take the role of debriefer and the preference is for each participant to have two attempts at this. The remainder of the participants either take the part of teams members or an individual returnee or observers. One of the two facilitators acts as an observer and helps the debriefer to think out loud about what they are doing and why.

A noticeable feature of the early stage of the training process once simulations are introduced is the difficulty participants have in making use of the material they have been given. Often participants in the early simulations will simply listen to what is being said as if it were a story which they have no part in. There is no effort to contain the session and no conscious tracking of the emerging dynamics. The facilitator continually has to interrupt the simulation to give the debriefer time to reflect and understand what is being said. Time is deliberately given to one simulation prior to lunch on the first day so that participants can see how it is done and reflect on the benefits. They then return for the first afternoon session which is a review of the material presented thus far.

During that session the facilitators take the participants through the dynamics that would be expected in returnees by rote until participants are reasonable fluent in them. Following that the remainder of the afternoon is devoted to simulations, generally giving each participant an extended period of time for debriefing (usually not more than 15 minutes). Scenarios can be extended or new ones brought in according to how the group is handling the material.

The final session of the afternoon is a brief reflection time on the course so far. Some participants report feelings of confusion and inadequacy. Others report beginning to internalise key ideas gained during the day. Many reflect the idea that debriefing is more of a disciplined activity than they had appreciated.

The first session of the second day commences with a question and answer session followed by further simulations. After coffee participants are then given the opportunity either to continue simulations or to devise their own debriefing programmes or outline policies for their particular situation.

The course in its early days ended at this point with a review and feedback. However it became clear that people normally needed time to reflect on rare but difficult issues and accordingly the course was extended to include an (optional) afternoon session for those issues. The issues covered vary but can include sessions on how to recognise Post Traumatic Stress Disorder and how to refer it on to the appropriate professionals or sessions on protocols that can be followed in the case of emergencies such as death on the field or serious conflict problems.

The final session is an evaluation of the course as a whole, in particular what the participants themselves feel they have gained from the course. Typical examples of comments are given in Table 5-3.

For many people the use of simulations, although at first threatening, was an intensely valuable part of the course. They were able to see briefing from both the debriefer's perspective and the debriefee's perspective and to think through, usually in some detail, the issues behind people's

Table 5-3
Summary of sample feedback from debriefing course participants

Helpful bits

- Used real situations – could relate to experiences and were really confronted with what it was like to do and experience debriefing
- Putting d/b in context of whole outreach – the interplay between briefing and the rest of the experience
- May come across individuals needing help – can use techniques with them.

Key things learnt

- Significance & importance of debriefing
- Trusting one's own feelings
- How to think & write at the same time
- Giving everyone a voice
- I don't have to make everything right or make things better
- Debriefing is not counselling
- Don't take on things that don't belong
- Don't have to get to the bottom of everything
- Value of group work
- Need to give time to debriefing
- Leave a gap – need to feel what it is like at home
- 6 areas of debriefing – putting things into categories
- Idea of grouping by length of service
- Briefing is crucial – debriefing as part of package

presentation on their return home. For others the idea of debriefing as an integral part of the outreach experience was a revelation. Most had viewed it either as an optional extra or as something to be done only in the case of emergency or difficulty.

YWAM as an agency tends to give priority to individuality when working on personal issues or team issues and so the idea of working through personal issues within a group setting is a novel one. There is also perhaps a tendency to want to explore issues in depth with people and to work with them in that rather than allowing them to work through their own solutions. The course emphasises healing or resolution happening extensively within the group with the facilitator being precisely that, a catalyst for change rather than a directive change agent. For lay people unused to the powerful dynamics that can be at work in groups this tends to be a novel and slightly threatening idea until they see the benefits of the dynamics involved. Following that there is a dawning recognition that the responsibility to 'make things better' or makes things 'all right' does not lie with the debriefer but rather is between the debriefee and God or, in secular settings, is the responsibility of the debriefee alone. The debriefer is simply there to validate and normalise the process in a context which provides credible social support.

The course outlined here is a straightforward way to introduce the key concepts of debriefing and to give people the skills they need for the routine debriefing of individuals or groups returning from abroad. The necessary components of the course, from the feedback we have so far, seem to be the use of simulations, running the course over two days, selling a particular method and keeping the group small enough for all to benefit directly.

---

[1] Gardner R., and Gardner L.M., *Training and using member care workers*, In O'Donnell, K., (Ed) Missionary Care, William Carey Library, California, 1992.

[2] Heather Wright was the author's co-leader for each course and much of the development of the course is due to her input.

[3] Davidson, S., *The People In Aid Code of Best Practice*, Relief and Rehabilitation Network Paper 20, London, 1997.

Chapter 6

Post Traumatic Stress Disorder

Description of Post Traumatic Stress Disorder and Acute Stress Disorder
Post Traumatic Stress Disorder (PTSD) or Post Traumatic Stress Syndrome (PTSS) can be thought of as a chronic and intense anxiety state which doesn't go away. Historically the names of this serious psychiatric problem have varied as has the treatment. Previously PTSD has been referred to as battle shock, battle fatigue or shell shock. Combat related prevalence rates have tended to be high. Treatment was the removal of those affected as quickly as possible from the battlefront to somewhere calm where, it was assumed, they would recover. Removal from the front line was also prioritised so that the morale of comrades would not be affected. In fact recovery rates were low and return rates to the front line were poor.

The source for much of the understanding of PTSD until recently was the literature generated by military psychiatrists and psychologists and concerned battle induced PTSD.[1] It was no coincidence that some of the civilian Lebanese Hostages released in 1991 were debriefed by military psychiatrists. Partly, it is true, intelligence gathering was required, equally however it was the military psychiatrists at that time who had the expertise to conduct such a debriefing.

Since then research into the condition has progressed along a number of fronts.[2,3] The first is identifying populations where PTSD can be identified. This helps to determine populations at risk and also populations where treatment may be indicated. Apart from military personnel exposed to combat, PTSD has been identified in the emergency services, in concentration camp survivors and in members of the general population caught up in serious catastrophes such as ferry sinkings and oil rig fires.

Research is continuing into defining PTSD. There has been broad agreement that PTSD exists as a unitary phenomenon since 1980[4] but the exact description has been refined twice since then[5] and the latest will be presented below.

The diagnostic criteria for PTSD have been refined in the latest, fourth, edition of the Diagnostic and Statistical Manual of the American Psychiatric Association (DSM-IV)[6] and the criteria are outlined in Table 6-1.

Criterion A has been adapted from previous editions of the Diagnostic and Statistical Manual so that a subjective element is added. Previous editions had held that exposure to a traumatic event was a necessary factor in experiencing PTSD. DSM-IV takes note of the person's response at the

Table 6-1
DSM-IV criteria for PTSD

A. The person has been exposed to a traumatic event in which both of the following were present:

(1) the person experienced, witnessed, or was confronted with an event or events that involved actual or threatened death or serious injury, or a threat to the physical integrity of self or others.
(2) the person's response involved intense fear, helplessness or horror.

B. The traumatic event is persistently re-experienced.

C. The person must persistently avoid stimuli associated with the trauma or experience a numbing of general responsiveness not present before the trauma.

D. The person must experience persistent symptoms of increased arousal not present before the trauma.

E. Symptoms must have lasted at least a month. The diagnosis is specified as acute if duration of the symptoms is less that three months and chronic if greater than three months. Delayed onset is specified if the onset of symptoms is at least six months after the stressor.

F. The disturbance causes clinically significant distress or impairment in social, occupational or other important areas of functioning.

time to account for the fact that not everyone experiencing a traumatic event becomes traumatised.[7] Table 6-2 outlines some of the possible stressors which can lead on to PTSD.

Criteria B – F in Table 6-1 outline the necessary symptoms for a diagnosis of PTSD. For a diagnosis of PTSD to be made the person must persistently re experience the event; avoid stimuli associated with the event or experience a numbing of general responsiveness and experience increased arousal. Symptoms must last at least a month. The disturbance must significantly impair the person's day to day functioning.

The definitions of re-experiencing, stimulus avoidance or numbing and

Table 6-2
DSM-IV examples of stressors leading to PTSD

- Military combat, violent personal assault, being kidnapped, being taken hostage, terrorist attack, torture, incarceration as a prisoner of war or concentration camp, natural or manmade disasters, severe car accidents, being diagnosed with a life threatening illness.
- Witnessing a serious injury or un-natural death of another or unexpectedly witnessing a dead body.
- Sudden destruction of one's environment.

increased arousal are outlined in Tables 6-3, 6-4 and 6-5 respectively.

Finally, research is progressing into the dynamics underlying PTSD and, given those dynamics, the natural progression of PTSD from cause to remission and the most effective treatments.

To date there is little published work at all on PTSD in the missionary

Table 6-3
Five ways in which the trauma may be re-experienced (criterion B). One or more must be present

B1. Recurrent and intrusive distressing recollections of the event including images thoughts or perceptions.

B2. Recurrent distressing dreams of the event.

B3. Acting or feeling as if the traumatic event were recurring (this includes a sense of reliving the experience, illusions, hallucinations, and dissociative (flashback) episodes including those that occur upon waking or when intoxicated).

B4. Intense psychological distress at exposure to internal or external cues that symbolise or resemble an aspect of the traumatic event.

B5. Physiological reactivity upon exposure to internal or external cues that symbolise or resemble an aspect of the traumatic event (for example a woman who was raped in a lift breaks out in a sweat when entering a lift).

> **Table 6-4**
>
> **Seven indicators of avoidance of numbing (Criterion C)**
> **Three or more must be present**
>
> C1. Efforts to avoid thoughts, feelings or conversations associated with the trauma
>
> C2. Efforts to avoid activities, places or people that arouse recollections of the trauma
>
> C3. Inability to recall an important aspect of the trauma (psychogenic amnesia)
>
> C4. Markedly diminished interest or participation in significant activities
>
> C5. Feelings of detachment or estrangement from others
>
> C6. Restricted range of affect, for example unable to have loving feelings
>
> C7. Sense of a foreshortened future, for example does not expect to have a career, marriage, children, or a normal life span

or aid agency population although the author is aware of some helpful work.[8][9][10] It is clear, however, from the clinical experience of those working with returning missionaries and aid workers that PTSD exists within both these populations.

A number of theoretical descriptions have been put forward to account

> **Table 6-5**
>
> **Five examples of increased arousal (criterion D)**
> **Two or more must be present**
>
> D1. Difficulty falling or staying asleep
>
> D2. Irritability or outbursts of anger
>
> D3. Difficulty concentrating
>
> D4. Hypervigilance
>
> D5. Exaggerated startle responses

for PTSD. A common theme throughout is the notion of otherwise ordinary people becoming psychologically overwhelmed by a highly abnormal experience. Not only their senses but also their abilities to process incoming information are overwhelmed and it is as if the normal mechanisms available simply jam or seize up. The events leading to the anxiety state are recalled in full detail over and over in their full original intensity. Normally, when replaying events that trouble us, the events are processed, put into context and steadily lose their intensity. In time they may become so absorbed that they are all but forgotten in everyday life. For those experiencing PTSD the memories of traumatic events are replayed but not processed, they do not diminish in intensity, they are not contextualised and they are certainly not forgotten.

The prognosis, without treatment, is bleak. Cases of PTSD have now been documented where people experience the disorder for many years without any improvement. They may be in such a state that going about everyday life is, in fact, impossible.

An acute, self limiting but incapacitating stress reaction can occur in the immediate aftermath of a traumatic incident. Termed Acute Stress Disorder (Combat Stress Reaction in the military[11]) the symptoms are similar in many ways to those of PTSD. (Table 6-6 next page). People experience dissociation from reality, re experience the traumatic event, avoid stimuli that arouse recollection of the trauma, are very anxious, distressed and socially impaired. The prevalence of ASR seems a direct function of proximity to a personally life threatening event and the effects are worsened if the support of colleagues or other social support is markedly diminished during the event for any reason.

The progress of the reaction is normally very fluid. Treatment at or near the site of the traumatic event is essential if at all possible. Those affected are encouraged to resume normal and adaptive functioning even if symptoms are still present. Those affected are encouraged to express their emotions as freely as possible so that the process of healing can occur. If left untreated then it is estimated that 30% – 40% of those experiencing ASR may go on to become incapacitated by, for example, PTSD.[12]

Where the reaction lasts longer than a month following the event the diagnosis is changed by definition to PTSD and a different treatment regimen is indicated.

Preventative Factors

Treatment of PTSD has been studied from a number of different perspectives but it has to be said that the best treatment is prevention and, to that end, there is a lot that is known about significantly reducing the risk of PTSD in at-risk populations. By contrast treatment for PTSD is inadequately understood, scarce and with limited efficacy although the situation is rapidly improving.

Table 6-6
Diagnostic criteria for Acute Stress Disorder (DSM IV)

A. The person has been exposed to a traumatic event in which both of the following were present:

(1) the person experienced, witnessed, or was confronted with an event or events that involved actual or threatened death or serious injury, or a threat to the physical integrity of self or others.
(2) the person's response involved intense fear, helplessness or horror.

B. Either while experiencing or after experiencing the distressing event the individual has three or more of the following dissociative symptoms:

1. a subjective sense of numbing, detachment, or absence of emotional responsiveness
2. a reduction in awareness of his or her surroundings (e.g. 'being in a daze')
3. derealisation
4. depersonalisation
5. dissociative amnesia

C. The traumatic event is persistently re-experienced in at least one of the following ways: recurrent images, thoughts, dreams, illusions, flashback episodes, or a sense or reliving the experience; or a distress on exposure to reminders of the traumatic event.

D. Marked avoidance of stimuli that arouse recollections of the trauma (e.g. thoughts, feelings, conversations, activities, places, people).

E. Marked symptoms of anxiety or increased arousal (e.g., difficulty sleeping, irritability, poor concentration, hypervigilance, exaggerated startle response, motor restlessness).

F. The disturbance causes clinically significant distress or impairment in social, occupational or other important areas of functioning or impairs the individual's ability to pursue some necessary task such as obtaining necessary assistance or mobilising personal resources by telling family members about the traumatic experience.

G. The disturbance lasts for a minimum of two days and occurs within four weeks of the traumatic event.

Several factors protective of developing PTSD have already been described in chapter 3. The most potent are those of consultative leadership and group or team cohesion. However other factors are also key. The easiest to apply are in the areas of selection, training and continuing support. Critical in all of this is the fact that those experiencing trauma will not necessarily go on to experience PTSD. It is now almost possible to say that the long term effects of traumatic situations can be reduced to vanishing point if the recommendations in the literature as it stands at the moment are implemented.

Protective selection criteria are reported in the literature in a very narrow way and it may be that recommendations will settle down to a more realistic level after further study. Currently the advice being given on the basis of the available literature to reduce the risk of PTSD is to reject anyone who has any history of any mental illness whatsoever. Those with a history of PTSD, even in remission, are considered particularly vulnerable. These recommendations are now publicly available and it is for individual agencies and team leaders to decide whether, or to what extent, to abide by them. It seems likely that these recommendations will be modified in the future. They are too broad and they are currently based on simple correlations between crude, global diagnoses ('depression', 'eating disorder') and the incidence of PTSD. In time, more helpful criteria will probably be generated which will more precisely take account of what it is within a history of mental illness that makes people vulnerable to PTSD. In the meantime assessment by a mental health professional is essential for those at high risk of encountering trauma who also have any history of mental health problems.

The selection criteria adopted for students and short term workers applying to the R&D training department in YWAM (UK) for placement overseas have been less stringent than those above. However, from over 140 graduates who have satisfied the criteria, none have been diagnosed with PTSD during the last six years despite a significant number being exposed to the sorts of stressors which could precipitate PTSD in a vulnerable population. The selection criteria are as follows:

1. No history of any psychotic disorder (e.g. schizophrenia, manic depression[13]).
2. No episodes of depression or anxiety within the previous two years. Candidates should have been off all medication for a period of two years.
3. No history of eating disorders within the previous five years.

The information is gleaned from candidates' self report and from references. In addition applications are also scrutinised for any discrepancy between self report and independent report with discrepancies followed up and/or the candidate rejected summarily from the application process.

It must be emphasised that the above criteria are designed to minimise the risk of people dropping out of training or service through a re-occurrence of a previous mental disturbance brought about by stress. Thus candidates may be accepted if their depression for example was unrelated to stressors they are likely to encounter in training or on the field. It is only incidentally protective of experiencing PTSD and considerably more research is required in the area.

Selection may also be made with respect to what has been termed resilience.[14] Rutter has defined resilience as 'residing in how people deal with life changes and what they do about their situation. That quality is influenced [by developmental experiences throughout life].' None of these is in itself determinate of later outcomes but in combination may serve to create a chain of indirect linkages that foster escape from adversity'. Where trauma ('combat') is encountered resilience is a 'moderately potent protective factor'.[15]

Training has many aspects to it but the most potent, with respect to PTSD prevention, is realistic professional training. There are a number of tentative theoretical reasons for this. Assuming that a major factor in onset of PTSD is cognitive overload then any way of reducing that load will facilitate processing of information. To that end practising and rehearsing routine tasks which are likely to accompany a traumatic event will mean that the novelty of those tasks will diminish, they will become more or less routine and automatic. As a consequence the amount of cognitive effort required to carry out the tasks will be markedly diminished. This will leave more processing capacity for the other aspects of the traumatic event and mean that the emotional and cognitive reconciliation processes are less likely to become stuck.

In practice for Aid workers this can mean conducting a number of simulated activities during training and a number of realistic activities during otherwise quiet parts of a field mission. Two examples may be given. In some traumatic situations anyone available may well be called upon to perform what are termed 'body handling' duties, a known PTSD inducing stressor. For medical staff already trained in such duties or used to the sight of blood, gore and death, body handling is unlikely to be a significant PTSD inducing stressor. For logisticians, engineers and support staff it is more likely to be such a stressor and thus training of the type given by national Red Cross associations for major disasters may help to diminish the stressful impact of such work. Evacuations are major stressors and, again, the impact can be diminished on site simply by practising the manoeuvres involved. There are many other examples from the relatively minor (how to use a fire extinguisher, how to drive a four wheel drive vehicle) to the major (what to do when the rebels attack). The side benefit of such training is that staff are more likely to be of use in a traumatic situation, are more likely to stay calm and more likely to be able to assist others.

For those on the field, or about to go, team formation or existing team dynamics are critical. From the military literature the presence of officers or NCO's (i.e. team leaders) with a consultative leadership style and the experience of good team cohesion precisely differentiates those people who become traumatised in a traumatically stressful situation from those who do not. For the purposes of traumatic stress reduction it is possible to further refine the definition of consultative leadership style. Those in charge need to lead by example, that is act out the kind of responses that will safeguard both physical and mental health, such as calm responses. Officers need to maintain objectivity and discipline when dealing with those in their charge – that is the soldiers need to feel treated fairly, justly and reasonably. The officer needs to know the soldiers personally – not intimately necessarily but certainly enough about them that the soldiers are more than just cogs in a machine. Those in charge need to be subject to the same adverse conditions as the men in their charge both in the every day activities of living as well as exposure to danger. Finally the leaders are willing to see to needs of their men before their own needs.[16]

Team cohesion has been discussed in chapter 3 together with the idea of social support. The definition of cohesion is further refined by other authors:

> The bonding together of (soldiers) in such a way as to sustain their will and commitment to each other, the unit [team] and mission [project], despite combat or mission stress.[17]

For trauma prevention some further factors seem essential. Team members need the ability to form work relationships, that is work co-operatively and harmoniously with others from the same team. Beyond that, team members need to be able to function within a team setting, not just when engaged in communal tasks but also when working alone and when off duty.

A further feature from the military literature needs discussion but it has profound implications for aid work and missionary work. Some distinction has been drawn between the protective features of the organisation of US armed forces and the organisation of UK armed forces. It appears that the US armed forces may have a heightened probability of experiencing PTSD because of the way soldiers are often moved around so they are continually having to establish new, trusting relationships. There is little identity with the corps of men to whom the soldier is attached and therefore little group loyalty or sense of belonging. This is contrasted with the British Regimental system where members of the regiment have a strong cultural identity and a high probability of knowing one another since they serve together in a more contained unit. To that end serving or working with a predictable, known group of people is demonstrably protective of PTSD. Aid workers in general and relief workers in particular have a very high turnover of colleagues and it seems probable that this would heighten the risk of a stress reaction. Therefore consideration needs to be given to the formation of reasonably stable groups of workers for multiple tours of duty in relief work rather than the current practice of simply putting people together, more or less at random, for varying lengths of time in different projects thus causing instability in the teams and significantly heightened vulnerability to PTSD.

Evidence is beginning to emerge of the role social support plays in helping survivors adjust back to normal functioning. Parkes[18] has suggested that the high rate of PTSD following a dam burst above the town of Buffalo Creek in the USA was partially due to the separation of survivors by the emergency services in the immediate aftermath of the tragedy. Flannery[19] takes the argument further by suggesting that social support plays four roles. Sharing feelings and being listened to provides emotional support; information as to the truth of the situation can be gleaned from others; feelings of loneliness, helplessness and vulnerability are reduced by social companionship and, finally, practical help can be provided.

A final factor is beyond the ability of agency staff to mitigate but is one of the most potent factors in the impact of a traumatic incident. The degree and intensity of exposure to trauma show a direct relationship to the intensity of PTSD in the military population but the picture is more confused in the civilian population.[20] Broadly, proximity to the event, duration of the event and the subjective horror of the event all contribute to its potency as a stressor.

Treatment

The practice of debriefing in the face of trauma, let alone as a routine exercise, is a comparatively recent phenomenon for civilians and the need for it can be questioned. In the UK Prince Philip has expressed contempt both for people receiving debriefing and for those offering it. As ever he touches a nerve. The British Newspaper 'The Independent' ran an article questioning the need for trauma debriefing in civilian populations.[21] A colleague of mine once attempted to discuss her debriefing work with a much older man. He was dismissive, pointing out that during the second world war both the military and the civilian population just 'got on with it'. "There was no counselling available and everyone seemed OK, therefore there is no need for counselling today" was his theory.

The man was wrong on several counts – everyone was not OK; trauma was labelled differently at that time (e.g. shell shock or battle fatigue) and poorly understood. Counselling was available but was labelled 'debriefing'. Equally the civilian population was not unaffected either. Many did become traumatised but those affected by trauma were hidden away in institutions. Others did not become traumatised as such but clearly carried the effects of the war with them for the rest of their life. In the UK there used to be a benign weekly television comedy about the Second World War. At the end of the programme, as the signature tune faded out, both my mother and many of her wartime friends would complain, every week, at the air raid siren noise that was faded in. This was during the 1970's.

The other factor not apparently taken into account is the very different social setting that pertained during the war, for example in London. During the Blitz entire neighbourhoods would be destroyed. People were not alone in their physical loss and emotional pain. Many hundreds of others had suffered the same way, that night. The natural inclination of people during such disasters is to come together in mutual support. The phenomenon of the 'Blitz spirit' is fondly remembered even amongst the horror of what was going on.

Today if a house is bombed in a terrorist attack or if there is a civilian disaster survivors are very much on their own. Civilian disaster survivors probably go through the traumatic event with people who live no where near them, thus obviating the possibility of future mutual support. On returning home they may be surrounded by people who have no possibility of remotely understanding what they have been through or what they are going through. If the theories are correct and PTSD is an acute anxiety state which has got stuck then the lack of social support can only contribute to that lack of progress. In the Blitz, people were together in their shared public tragedy; in today's modern world, comparatively free of trauma, people are on their own in their personal private tragedy.

This is not a treatment manual and is not designed to enable people to conduct the psychotherapeutic treatment of those experiencing a very serious disorder.[22][23] Nevertheless there are things which can be done on the field. There is broad agreement on the nature of the approach to those experiencing PTSD. What follows then is an overall description of a form of self debriefing for situations where outside help is unavailable followed by an overview of the approaches used for those who go on to experience difficulties.

Critical Incident Stress Debriefing (CISD)[24] is usually conducted by a trained counsellor in the 48 hours or so following a traumatic ('critical') incident. It has a number of components. The introductory phase lays the ground rules for what is to come – everyone has an equal voice, everything said is confidential. Participants are told of the need to attend all sections of the debrief. In the next phase each participant talks through their experiences in four sections – what happened, what they thought, how they reacted and what they felt. Following that, teaching is given by the debriefer to describe and account for their likely reactions and to make suggestions for potential coping strategies. At the end participants talk through how they personally can best cope as they leave.

With the possible addition of an explicit section on spirituality much of the above method can be applied on the field, preferably with a credible outsider, preferably one known to the group.

The drawback is that the method was designed for rescue workers who may experience very few critical incidents. Missionaries and aid workers by contrast may experience many critical incidents during each tour of duty and it is unlikely that managers will be willing to pull staff off duty for up to six hours or so each time, for example, a refugee camp is shelled, there is an armed hold-up or a vehicle is hijacked. One team in Grozny, for example, experienced three critical incidents in the ten days or so prior to being evacuated, itself a potential critical incident.

Given that, much trauma debriefing practice does share a number of commonalties. It is normally done soon after the traumatic event, usually on site or nearby. Debriefing is a group activity involving both cognitive activity and a factual review and input. The result is often re-framing of previously held views and the learning of new information. There is some debate over the timing of the debriefing and whether all those who have been exposed to trauma need debriefing. Here practice is in advance of theory. Recent evidence shows no advantage for debriefing people immediately after a trauma, on the contrary there is some evidence that it may be counter productive. Some research also suggests that only those experiencing symptoms after a month need to be debriefed.

Debriefing however is a complex dynamic although not a complex technique. The evidence is unequivocal that the credibility of a debriefer is central to the recovery process as outlined in chapter 4. Credibility has been defined in a number of ways but the essential factors are that the debriefer is perceived to understand what the debriefees are describing by virtue of having had the same, or a least very similar, experiences. It therefore seems possible that what are normally referred to as non-specific therapeutic variables (e.g. the personality of the therapist) are actually of central importance. Certainly in my experience I am 'credible' if I have visited a team on site and then go on to debrief team members. I am less credible if they do not perceive me as having gone through the same experiences as them or of having been to the same places.

For those who do go on to experience PTSD there are few specialist resources currently available. The quality of the resource needed is outlined in a recent scientific paper.[25] A twelve day residential course with some 63 hours of structured sessions for between 4 and 8 patients was described. Two therapists and a support therapist were involved. Intervention included medication where indicated, group discussion, teaching, problem solving and reintegration of patients with their families. Most clients improved as a result and the improvement was maintained at a 12 month follow up.

It is clear that PTSD is a significant but preventable risk factor for those serving overseas as missionaries and aid workers. From the above it is equally clear that agencies can have access to a knowledge base which will enable them to select out people who are at heightened risk of PTSD in the presence of trauma. Beyond that, realistic professional training will help to reduce the risk further. Leadership training and active attention to the group dynamics of cohesion and social support reduce the risk to vanishing point.

Despite this lowered risk it seems probable that agency workers experiencing trauma should have a chance to talk through their experiences within the agency framework, on site as quickly as possible after each and every event. There is no doubt that workers should be monitored for PTSD after a traumatic event and those experiencing significant symptoms one month or more after the critical incident should be offered or referred to expert psychiatric help. The nature of that help is likely to take the form of a brief intervention in a group setting. PTSD need not be viewed as a psychiatric condition but rather a temporary failure of an individual's mind to process a traumatic event which is subjectively overwhelming. To that end the method of trauma debriefing is less to do with psychotherapy and counselling and more to do with retraining and facilitating peoples' natural but jammed resources to process their memories of the event. With the appropriate skilled, credible and group based help the recovery prognosis is good.

[1] Gal, R., and Mangelsdorff, A.D. (Eds) (1991) *Handbook of Military Psychology.* Chichester: John Wiley.
[2] Joseph, S., Williams R., Yule W., (1996) *Understanding Post Traumatic Stress.* Chichester, John Wiley.
[3] Scott M.J., Stradling S.G., *Counselling for Post Traumatic Stress Disorder,* (1992) London : Sage.
[4] APA (1980) *Diagnostic and Statistical Manual (3rd Ed)* (DSM III) Washington, American Psychiatric Association.
[5] APA (1987 and 1994) *DSM III-R and DSM-IV,* Washington, American Psychiatric Association.
[6] APA (1994) op cit.
[7] Busuttil, W., Interventions in PTSS, Implications for military and emergency service organisations, 1995, Unpublished M. Phil. Thesis, University of London states that only 25% – 52% of people experiencing trauma will go on to develop PTSD.
[8] Lovell, D.M. Psychological Adjustment amongst returned overseas aid workers, Unpublished D. Clin Psy Thesis, University of Wales, Bangor, 1997.
[9] Carr, K., Trauma and post-traumatic stress among missionaries. Evangelical Missions Quarterly, Vol 30, 1994, 246-255.
[10] Carr, K., Crisis intervention for missionaries, *Evangelical Missions Quarterly,* Vol 33, 1997, 450-458.
[11] Noy, S., Combat Stress Reactions, In Gal and Mangelsdorf op cit. is a useful source of information in this whole area.
[12] Soloman, R.L. and Benbenishty, R., The role of proximity, immediacy and expectancy in the front-line treatment of combat stress reaction amongst Israelis in the Lebanon war. *American Journal of Psychiatry,* 1986, **143**, 613-617.
[13] Bi polar depression in the USA.
[14] Rutter. M., Resilience in the Face of adversity: Protective factors and resistance to psychiatric disorder. *British Journal of Psychiatry,* 1985, **147**, 598-611. P 608: quoted in Busuttil (1995) op cit.
[15] Busuttil (1995) op cit.

[16] Busuttil (1995) op cit.
[17] Meyer quoted in Gal et al 1991 op cit.
[18] Parkes, C.M. Planning for the aftermath, *Journal of the Royal Society of Medicine*, 1991, **84**, 22-25.
[19] Flannery, R.B. Social Support and Psychological Trauma: a Methodological Review. *Journal of Traumatic Stress,* 1990, **3**, 593-611.
[20] Busuttil (1995), op cit.
[21] Ian Burrell, 'Doubts grow over trauma therapy', London, *The Independent*, 21st October 1996.
[22] O'Donnell K., Member Care Resource Guide, *Evangelical Missions Quarterly*, 1996, 32, 72- 79 is an invaluable guide to resources available around the word for the support of missionaries. It has been updated in Taylor, W.D. *Too Valuable to Lose*, William Carey Library, Pasadena, 1997.
[23] Shalev, A.H., Debriefing following trauma In Individual and Community responses to trauma and disaster: the structure of human chaos (Ed's R.J. Ursano et al,) pp 201 – 219. Cambridge: Cambridge University Press, 1994.
[24] Mitchell, J., and Everly, G., *Critical Incident Stress Debriefing: An Operations Manual for the prevention of traumatic stress amongst emergency services and disaster workers*. Ellicott City, Md., Chevron Publishing Corporation, 1993.
[25] Busuttil, W., et al, Incorporating Psychological Debriefing Techniques within a Brief Group Psychotherapy Programme for the Treatment of PTSD. *British Journal of Psychiatry*, 1995, **167**, 495-502.

Chapter 7

The question of suffering

1. INTRODUCTION

The issue of suffering in this world is one which many aid workers and missionaries seem to struggle with. This chapter is for three groups of people – those who are about to go out, perhaps for the first time. It is also for those for whom the issue of suffering has stopped simply being of academic interest and has become 'real' or 'alive' as a result of what they have seen and experienced overseas. Finally, those who are preparing others for the rigours of missionary service or aid work may find the following ideas helpful as a practical theology and framework for teaching. Logically and emotionally the question of suffering has to be faced with due humility. As one historian has said 'Any answer to the question of suffering has to be acceptable in the face of a dying child'.[1]

For me the issue is real on two counts. My personal and private life has taken me into many areas of the suffering of others over the last twenty years and I have also had my own share of personal pain. Trite answers to suffering stopped being adequate a long time ago. However, as a trainer, I find my personal answers are all very well but frequently do not satisfy others. I have watched many dear people lose their faith after their overseas experiences, overwhelmed by the discrepancy between the God they thought they knew and the pain they saw in or around others. My desire has therefore been, during training courses, to give people an adequate grasp of the essentials of a theology of suffering which would free them up to see God for themselves in the midst of turmoil.

Academic theology on its own, however, is not enough. It has to be grounded in a living faith and relationship with God otherwise it is so much dross. I am not, therefore, attempting a systematic theology which will provide clear answers but rather trying to provide a useful platform from which people can begin to ask their own questions of the Lord. In doing that I shall look at five issues. Mystery or how it is that Christ can be present in suffering; God's sovereign will and God's Kingdom; God's sovereignty and God's character; Displacement – our personal place in suffering. I end with a brief outline of coping with suffering.

It is important that we don't just wander in to the topic. As we continue we shall see that to study this topic is to study the very heart of the Christian faith and the very Holiness of God.

Interlude 1 – a true story
The civil war started again in Liberia. In the midst of it nuns sought to care for orphans in an institution by the beach. One day the fighters came. The nuns and many of the children were from the wrong tribe and were to be shot.

The passage of scripture central to this chapter is Philippians 2:1-18

1 If you have any encouragement from being united with Christ, if any comfort from his love, if any fellowship with the Spirit, if any tenderness and compassion,
2 then make my joy complete by being like-minded, having the same love, being one in spirit and purpose.
3 Do nothing out of selfish ambition or vain conceit, but in humility consider others better than yourselves.
4 Each of you should look not only to your own interests, but also to the interests of others.
5 Your attitude should be the same as that of Christ Jesus:
6 Who, being in very nature God, did not consider equality with God something to be grasped,
7 but made himself nothing, taking the very nature of a servant, being made in human likeness.
8 And being found in appearance as a man, he humbled himself and became obedient to death—even death on a cross!
9 Therefore God exalted him to the highest place and gave him the name that is above every name,
10 that at the name of Jesus every knee should bow, in heaven and on earth and under the earth,
11 and every tongue confess that Jesus Christ is Lord, to the glory of God the Father.
12 Therefore, my dear friends, as you have always obeyed— not only in my presence, but now much more in my absence— continue to work out your salvation with fear and trembling,
13 for it is God who works in you to will and to act according to his good purpose.
14 Do everything without complaining or arguing,
15 so that you may become blameless and pure, children of God without fault in a crooked and depraved generation, in which you shine like stars in the universe
16 as you hold out the word of life—in order that I may boast on the day of Christ that I did not run or labour for nothing.
17 But even if I am being poured out like a drink offering on the sacrifice and service coming from your faith, I am glad and rejoice with all of you.
18 So you too should be glad and rejoice with me.

2. MYSTERY – THE PLACE OF CHRIST IN SUFFERING

Mother Theresa of Calcutta said that by tending the wounded we tend the wounds of Christ. This assertion finds support in Matthew. 25:31-46. Christ speaks in the passage of people being judged on the extent to which they helped suffering people. However Christ explicitly has the judge identify himself with those who are suffering – 'whatever you did for the least of these you did for me'.

Therein lies one of the central mysteries of suffering. In order to understand the richness of this we need to understand something of the meaning of the word 'mystery'. In modern, enlightenment times the word has come to mean that which is not understood rationally. The disappearance of people from the Marie Celeste is described as a mystery because it cannot be understood rationally. Similarly suffering is described as a mystery because it cannot be explained rationally and to people's satisfaction. Yet the word has a much deeper and richer meaning theologically which is more to do with paradox or epigram.

Scripture is a clear example. The Bible is considered to be fully Divine, inspired by God, the authoritative Word which Christ described as Himself. Yet the book, clearly, is also fully human. It is written on paper, it has been edited, its very content decided by committee.[2] Scripture is fully divine, yet fully human – how can that be? It can't, it is a mystery.

Similarly with the Cross we see the fully divine, fully human Christ hanging on an evil cross which was to become a sign of triumph. How can that be? It can't, it is a mystery.

In considering suffering we come across a similar form of mystery. To Mother Teresa and to the judge in Matthew 25 suffering is fully evil and to be abhorred. Yet, in the midst of the evil of suffering, Christ is present. He is said to be incarnate in the suffering or present in its very substance. Christ, fully divine, present in that which is evil and to be rejected. How can that be? It can't, it is a mystery.

Perhaps here we have the first clue as to what may go wrong when people confront suffering in its fullness for the first time. Over the last decades there has been much talk of spiritual warfare – the idea that a significant part of our prayer life should be battle with the enemy. By and large this idea can be defended both in scripture and in the life of the church down the ages. I think though that it has encouraged a wrong sense of the location of Christ. We would agree that Christ is present in us through the gift of the Holy Spirit. There is little sense in Charismatic theology of Christ being present in the wider world. Somehow the idea has caught on that Christ is present in us and only in us as the Church. As a result when we go 'out' we go out into a world of darkness taking the light of Christ with us. The problems emerge when we somehow have a sense of the light dimming or even being extinguished as our prayers to relieve the suffering of a refugee camp or a war zone or to see a local Christian church established do not seem to be answered. We battle with the powers of darkness which may or may not be present, yet do not address the suffering Christ in the midst of the horror.

For many, such unanswered prayer or apparent injustice can be one route to a deep seated crisis of faith. The loss of faith however is subtle. There is often less of a sense of loss of God, more a sense of frustration that their informal, personal theology no longer works. They become agnostic rather than atheistic. The theology which worked in the West no longer serves them elsewhere. It is as if they haven't lost faith in the existence of God but rather lost faith in their theology. The crisis is often accentuated by the stunning lack of humility of some of what passes for bible teaching. The orator declares from (invariably) his platform that what is being said is the inspired word of God, the Truth and goes on to declare God's absolute sovereignty coupled with an appeal for faith. There is no room for doubt or dissension. People believe and are happy to have the certainty. Then, on the field, what has been claimed to be the indisputable truth suddenly isn't and the missionary may have little capacity to think and pray through alternatives.

From Philippians 2:1 – 18 we can see that Christ is already incarnate in suffering. The point that we can glean from Philippians is that we are called to be like Christ in His suffering. That is to be the incarnation of Christ in the midst of a suffering and evil world, the burden of which Christ has already taken on His shoulders.

Pope John Paul II writes[3]

> God is not someone who remains only outside of the world, content to be in Himself all knowing and omnipotent. His wisdom and omnipotence are placed, by free choice, at the service of creation. If suffering is present in the history of humanity one understands why His omnipotence was manifested in the omnipotence of humiliation on the Cross. The scandal of the Cross remains the key to the interpretation of the great mystery of suffering, which is so much a part of the history of mankind.

Even contemporary critics of Christianity are in agreement on this point. Even they see that the crucified Christ is proof of God's solidarity with man in his suffering. God places Himself on the side of man. He does so in a radical way:

Phil 2:7-8 but made himself nothing, taking the very nature of a servant, being made in human likeness.
8 And being found in appearance as a man, he humbled himself and became obedient to death—even death on a cross!

Christ is present in suffering. He was there before we were even conceived, He is there now and, until He returns, He will be there long after we have gone. No wonder God has prepared good works in advance for us (Ephesians 2:10). As we approach suffering perhaps we need to have our eyes less focused on the evil that may or may not be present and more focused on our worship of the living Christ in our prayers and actions. He asks us to show the world Himself by entering (being baptised) into His suffering.

Interlude 2
The nuns and all the children were led out on to the beach. Even in the midst of war the fighters were aware of the need for an easy life. It is simpler to dig a mass grave in sand than elsewhere. The children were terrified yet calmed by the nuns. The nuns knelt and began to pray as the fighters lifted their guns to shoot.

3. GOD'S SOVEREIGN WILL AND GOD'S KINGDOM
There is a well known and now classic conundrum:

'In the face of the suffering of the world God is either all powerful but doesn't care or all loving but powerless'.[4]

There are other, hidden questions that arise when considering the sovereignty of God.

- Are we currently involved in the exercise of the authority of God?
- How does God know the future?
- Does God change His mind?
- Do we have free will only when it suits God?

Each of these questions will be examined as they stand citing the scriptural evidence and also the underlying problems that each question poses. Following that, a possible working solution is outlined concerning God's sovereign will and His actions.

A. Are we currently involved in the exercise of the authority of God?
Historically from scripture we can see that we are not a necessary part of the practice of God's authority. One example suffices, that of Creation. God created the universe without involving humans at all. In fact humans were the last thing created just to underscore the point. In human history people may be redundant in the exercise of sovereign authority. The Ten Commandments were given to Moses without the benefit of his input either in terms of drafting them or requesting them in the first place. It is

clear that, if we are involved in the exercise of God's authority, we need to look for examples where God chooses to involve us. It appears we cannot demand or expect involvement. There are three mechanisms by which God appears to involve us: prayer, obedient service and Incarnational lifestyle.

Prayer is referred to again below and is clearly expected of us. We are asked to worship God and to bring our prayers before Him, to ask forgiveness and so forth. Yet prayer is not always answered directly. Worship may be offered but be unacceptable because of sin (e.g. Amos 5:22), prayers may be offered but be rejected because of hypocrisy (e.g. Luke 18:9-14 – the prayers of the tax man and the Pharisee). Thus the act of worship and praying, in themselves, are not a necessary route to God exercising His authority.

Obedient service is expected of us, yet it is a very weak route for God to exercise authority if He is relying on frail humans gifted with free will. We may refuse, we may agree but later change our mind, we may not hear in the first place (e.g. the parable of the seeds, parable of people who differentially obeyed). A few hear and also act.

Incarnational lifestyle draws people to Christ because they see Christ in us. Peace comes to the house we visit, justice and truth prevail where we go, harmony is evident in the home, in the church, in the team, in the ministry. Yet the Incarnational lifestyle is often missed in the trappings of our ideas about that lifestyle.

An acquaintance once described her 'gift' of hospitality. She purchased candles, beautiful place settings and the finest food. The house was to be cleaned, almost disinfected, whenever a guest, by prior appointment, was to arrive. Children, husband, cat and dog were all washed, scrubbed and, as appropriate, de-infested of whatever might offend. The great day would arrive and the guest would enter to gentle music, pleasant conversation and, presumably, the joy of the hostess as her 'gift'.

Someone I never met before and am unlikely to meet again once gave me a cup of chai from a cracked George IV cup in a cockroach and rat infested mud hut at no notice. Through an interpreter we spoke of the weather, the price of chickens and how well kept the village was. I got up at the end of one of the most enjoyable tea parties of my life aching from the discomfort of the disintegrating chair I had been sitting on and thanking my host fervently for his hospitality as I put the cup down on the tea chest with a handkerchief for a table cloth on it. 'Praise God' said my host, and I did. On the way out a live chicken was thrust into my hand. We were unable to stay for dinner so we had a take away. Hospitality was not mentioned once but the fruit of the gift was evident.

Prayers which may or may not be answered, disobedient servants and servants who miss the point. The question perhaps is less to do with the lack of advancement of God's rule and more curiosity about how, on earth, it advances at all. It seems God wants us involved, it seems we want to be involved, it seems the two don't always meet.

B. How does God know the future?

Here we are concerned with whether God has the ability to know the future in some predictive way, whether He has an exhaustive knowledge of all possible futures or whether, in fact, He has only a partial knowledge of the future.

If God knows the future then the problem of his apparent lack of sovereignty worsens. If He is able to know the future then why does He not, in His omnipotence, prevent the wickedness that occurs? No human could predict Rwanda yet, presumably, God could, if indeed He can see the future. So why didn't he prevent it. Why didn't he prevent the births of Stalin, Hitler, Pol Pot and others? A more subtle problem with seeing into the future also exists. If God can see the future then the future is, in some way, predictable, that is to say fixed or predetermined. If that is the case then God is helpless anyway since there is only one fixed future and God cannot intervene. If the future is fixed then we are helpless puppets cast adrift on a stream of time, doomed to act out the roles that time dictates without the chance to change or, even, to know if change has occurred.

The question of prayer then becomes a recursive problem. The point of prayer, presumably at least in part, is to see current or future circumstances changed. If the future is fixed then what is the point of prayer? If we pray and God appears to answer then perhaps that is what the future held all along anyway – so why bother? If we pray and God appears not to answer then, presumably, that is also because the future is fixed. Not only that but our very act of praying is, itself, fixed in the flow of time. An immutable future wins either way.

Given the question the way it is, scripture appears to confuse us rather than illuminate. It is possible to find scriptural evidence for both the positions that God does and does not know the future. That the future is knowable is easily demonstrated from the prophecies concerning the birth and life of Christ and the prophecies of Christ himself. From these passages it seems clear that there is a future which it is possible to know about accurately.

Equally there are passages suggesting that some aspects of the future are not known even to some parts of the Godhead. The return of Christ is known only to the Father, not even to Christ. The outcome of the story of Job is unknown both to Satan and, apparently, to God.

The picture is confused. There seems to be a knowable future yet God does not always seem aware of it. If indeed there is a knowable (i.e. fixed) future then how is it that we claim to have free will? Is there any evidence that the future is indeed fixed so far as God is concerned in His sovereignty? This leads us on to the question of whether God can and does change His mind.

C. Does God change His mind?

Again scripture is equivocal when the question is put like this. It is possible to find evidence both that God does not change His mind and also that He does. The prayer of Daniel (Daniel 9) is one of the clearest examples of prayer being answered through God changing his mind. A further change of mind is spelt out in Jeremiah 16:19

> 19 ..... And did not the LORD relent, so that he did not bring the disaster he pronounced against them? ....

Yet we also understand God to be unchangeable and unchanging. The two clear 'proof' texts of this are in the Old Testament:

> Numbers 23:19 God is not a man, that he should lie, nor a son of man, that he should change his mind. Does he speak and then not act? Does he promise and not fulfil?

> 1 Samuel 15:29 He who is the Glory of Israel does not lie or change his mind; for he is not a man, that he should change his mind.

How can someone be both changeable and not changeable at the same time? How can someone both keep His promises and also change his mind about them?

Interlude 3

The nuns prayed to bless the fighters and their families. The fighters left, humbled by the prayers. The nuns and the children returned to the orphanage whilst, around them, the civil war continued and the numbers massacred rose hourly.

D. Do we have free will only when it suits God?

The issue of whether we have free will at all can be addressed scripturally. Implicit in the story of Job is his freedom to act. He was even free to choose to curse God or not and the spiritual forces were not allowed to intervene. Throughout the Pentateuch the Israelites referred to 'freewill' offerings, those offerings made of their own volition rather than in response to the Law (e.g. Exodus 31:29, Exodus 36:3). In Joshua the Israelites are given the free choice to serve God or other gods (Joshua 24:15). God explicitly asks people to choose (Deuteronomy 1:13). Clearly throughout the Old Testament free will is assumed and taken to be not only the ability of humans but also approved of by God. In the New Testament the writers speak extensively of freedom from sin and freedom from the law. In verses such as Galatians 5:1 it is clear that our freedom includes free will choice.

However scripture also makes it clear that God has a hand in our choices at times. We may choose but God may seek to be a part of the outcome. For example in Hosea 8:4 God complains that He has not approved the choice of the Israelites for King. God does not, here, complain that the Israelites made a choice, rather that they did not involve God in that choice.

The issue of free will becomes more complex when we see in many places in the New Testament reference being made to God choosing us (e.g. John 15:16, 1 Peter 1:2 and 2:9) and in the Old Testament choice being limited (e.g. Deuteronomy 12:5).

The issue of free will is central to understanding the problem of suffering. Above we can see that God has given humans the capacity for free will and allows free will to be exercised. In the parable of the wheat and tares we see that He allows the exercise of that free will in the short term so that the good things may flourish as well. Yet there is also evidence that our free will is not entirely unlimited. There are several ways in which this is true.

My choices cannot overcome natural circumstances. I may choose passionately to walk on the ceiling but gravity will intervene irrespective of my freedom to exercise choice.

My choices have consequences. If I choose to walk off a tall building certain things will follow. If I choose to sin then, again, there are consequences. God has given us the capacity to see the consequences of our actions and to modify our actions accordingly.

God makes choices. The nature and extent of those choices has been the stuff of debate ever since the Bible was written. We may respond to those choices freely, He does not force the choices upon us. Nevertheless circumstances come upon us where the obvious way ahead may be heavily limited.

In the New Testament we are encouraged to use our freedom for good – to worship and serve God and, even if our actions are not intrinsically wicked, to curtail them if, by continuing, we cause a brother to stumble. Choice is applauded but it is choice exercised responsibly.

There is therefore evidence in scripture that free will may be fully exercised, exercised within limits and exercised within very narrow limits set by God. We are not free to do anything – created nature prevents that. We are also aware that our actions have consequences. In the very long run our actions have the ultimate consequence of Christ's judgement.

When thinking about these issues and many other similarly tricky ones I am reminded of cameras which adjust their focus manually by bringing two small circles into alignment with each other. If the camera is out of focus then the circles are out of alignment, if the camera is in focus then one only sees one circle in the viewfinder. If one looks through the viewfinder and sees two circles and a blurry picture one does not declare the camera broken and discard it, rather one adjusts the camera to bring things into focus. It is similar with the kind of difficulty outlined above. The problem with the apparently inconsistent answers lies not with the solutions but with the questions themselves. As is well known in philosophy asking the wrong questions will result in meaningless, confusing or contradictory answers. We therefore have to adjust the questions we are asking rather than struggling to refine the contradictory answers.

Take the initial conundrum – 'God is either all powerful and doesn't care or is all loving but powerless'. The solution we want is that God is all powerful and all loving. The nightmare is that He doesn't care and is powerless as well. There are a number of things wrong with the assumptions underlying the conundrum before we even begin to set about solving it. It assumes that the attributes of power and love are all there is to the Christian understanding of God. Yet we know that other features exist as well. There is an additional assumption implicit in the conundrum that God will exercise his power, mainly for our benefit, in some way or another. A third assumption is that God is the only volitional agent at work in the created universe. Once those assumptions are made clear we begin to see that trying to solve the conundrum is actually a waste of effort since it is based on false premises.

Similar problems exist with the apparently straightforward question of whether God knows the future. Laying aside the issue of God's existence in eternity[5] it is clear that the question is too vague otherwise a clearer answer than 'yes and no ' or 'sort of' would emerge. None of the answers offered so far are satisfactory since they appear either contradictory or do not accord with our 'common sense' experience:

The solution that is proposed here is broadly known as the Arminian approach[6] and is to be contrasted with the approach of the theologian Calvin. A starting point for understanding this approach is the idea that God is all powerful and all loving but has *chosen*, in some ways been obliged, to limit Himself. He is limited through being true to His character, by acting on the prayers of the saints, by the free will He has given people and by the results of The Fall.

Interlude 4
The next day the fighters returned, drunk. Determined to carry out their orders. Again the nuns and children were led out to the beach. Again the nuns knelt. Again the guns were raised. This time the fighters would not stop.

4. GOD'S SOVEREIGNTY EXERCISED THROUGH HIS CHARACTER

A more honest approach to the question of sovereignty and the apparent lack of it is to ask the question 'Why Doesn't God always act as we expect him to'? We can sometimes have a view of God as a cosmic Santa Claus, more or less at our beck and call. Prayers are offered to be answered. If they are prayed in faith or fervently then the effort is more likely to be rewarded. Any lack of result is accounted for by wrong timing, lack of faith or personal sin. Little active consideration is given to the notion that God might have a view on the subject.

C. S. Lewis has been described by Tim Ware[7] as the closest writer to the Christian Orthodox tradition that the UK has. In Lewis's Narnia chronicles he has one of the characters exclaim of Aslan the Lion who represents Christ:

'He's not a tame Lion you know'.

Indeed He is not. He is described throughout the bible as the Sovereign LORD, someone to whom we go in awe. Christ operationalised the relationship when teaching the disciples how to pray in Matthew 6:10 '.....your Will be done....'. There is no suggestion anywhere in scripture that the Lord is there to do our bidding. Prayers of the form 'God do X' with a polite 'please' added as a mark of respect can smack more of magic than intercession or supplication.

It does seem clear that the balance to this is the relationship we have with the Lord, one of a loving father delighting to give good gifts to His children. However in that relationship we are encouraged to try to have the mind of Christ, to understand God's will in a situation and then to pray that into being.

This is hard. We long in our thoughts and actions and prayers to make things better. Sometimes that cannot be. I remember well the death from cancer of a highly respected and faithful YWAM worker. The local YWAM community prayed for her healing and many believed that would happen. It didn't and she died. Yet the understanding came that she was in a much better place and, beyond that, the Lord wanted her home. Who were we to hang on to her?

Years prior to this incident I suffered badly from nosebleeds. The least jolt or excitement would set off an uncontrollable bleed which could take many moments to stop. I was actively considering going to the doctor to try to sort something out. My wife and I had a Christian research psychology colleague to stay. As she came down stairs to breakfast I was in front of the hall mirror trying to sort out yet another bleed. In passing she briefly touched me and said 'Oh for heaven's sake you don't have to put up with that – Lord please stop these nosebleeds'. Two research psychologists looked at one another briefly thinking 'that was bold' then our friend asked where the cornflakes were and we got on with the day. It was some weeks before it dawned on me that my nosebleeds had stopped completely and a year before I was convinced I was not going to have another one.

One woman not healed of incurable terminal cancer; one man healed of a curable, trivial, medical condition. We are led inevitably to Isaiah 55:

> 8 'For my thoughts are not your thoughts, neither are your ways my ways,' declares the LORD.

God is mystery, both in the sense of being beyond rational thought and also mystery in the sense of being beyond our ability to understand fully. Beyond that He is eternal, we are temporal.

In all of this mystery, however, God has to be true to Himself. There are certain fundamental, unchangeable things that we know about Him. God is Love, Truth, Justice and so on. He is a good God and strongly desires good things for His children.

The minister of Dunblane Cathedral in Scotland spoke powerfully along these lines after sixteen children were shot dead in the town.

> 'Let no one commit the heresy of asking whether this was God's fault. It wasn't. God's heart was the first to break when the first bullet entered the first child'.

If we want to attach blame for evil then we have to look somewhere other than God. God's heart must have broken for many different reasons. Imagine the pain however of a deity who has the capacity to stop such a thing yet is impotent because of the promises He has made. A central promise is the gift of our free will enabling us to worship God of our own volition in Spirit and in Truth.

John Paul II put it thus "confronted with our human freedom, God decided to make Himself 'impotent'". This fact is made plain in the way Christ 'impotently' accepted suffering on the Cross and even echoed the same words of all who suffer – 'My God, My God why have you forsaken me'? In going through the suffering that He did He remained true to Himself – 'God is Love'.

God has made an ordered universe and within it placed people who have free will. Gravity, light and other fundamental 'rules' work well and predictably. There are consequences to our actions and God does not alter those consequences for our convenience. Gravity is not suspended if we walk off a cliff. Bullets will harm whatever gets in their way. Giving a gun to a madman and allowing him near children will have consequences. It is our responsibility, not God's, to ensure such things don't happen. For an all powerful deity to assume responsibility would allow us to abdicate all our responsibility, our free will would be curtailed or eliminated and we would become puppets.

As may quickly be deduced, the problem of miracles is not why more of them don't occur but rather how God allows any to occur at all. A key factor in them for the argument here, it seems, is their very unreliability and unpredictability. To repeat Lewis's words – 'He's not a tame Lion you know'.

Yet the pain of the gift of free will goes far beyond a consequential universe. Gerald Priestland wrote:

> 'I have been obsessed also with the love of God in the supreme gift of free will, and with the consequence of that loving gift being the inevitability of sin'.[8]

God's heart was the first to break long before bullets began to fly at all. He trusted us not to sin with the gift of free will which he had given to us to worship Him. We sinned and continue to sin and not only we but also an omnipotently powerless God must suffer the consequences. We suffer sometimes through our stupidity, sometimes through our actions, sometimes just because. God always, at all times, in all circumstances chooses to remain in the place of suffering when faced with our sin. He must be true to Himself. And we dare, at times, to ask Him 'why' or, even, to blame him. No wonder God is often silent in the face of such heresy.

God has also limited Himself through the prayers of the saints. We co-operate with God and He co-operates with us in the outworking of His divine will. Much has already been written elsewhere about prayer and this is not the place to add to that. It is sufficient to say that the sovereign will of God is bounded by the nature and extent of the prayers we offer.

Finally, we understand that the Fall itself had consequences. Evil came into the world and we were cast out from the presence of God. The Fall caused problems not just in mankind's relationship with God but also the whole of creation's relationship. To repeat, we live in a universe where our actions have consequences. What we see around us is not what God intended. Ever since the Fall God has been working to restore His Kingdom.

The question of our own personal protection inevitably arises. The most fundamental sense in which we are protected has nothing to do with this life at all but rather the eternal life to come. As a colleague of mine once said of recently facing a rebel with a gun – 'facing death was the easy bit, I was more concerned that it wouldn't hurt too much'. For Christians, facing death is straightforward, or at least can be. We are already protected from the worst that death can do to us.

Is there any sense then in which we are protected in this life? Scripture often suggests there is no protection against harm in this life, on the contrary, it is to be expected on two counts. Jesus suggested strongly that the coming of the Kingdom of God would be preceded by terrible things (Mark 13). Prior to that however he indicated that the life of a disciple of his would not be easy either. In Mark 10:29 He promises immediate reward for those who give up everything to follow Him. He adds that those who do follow Him can also expect persecution. This was certainly Paul's experience as he reports in 2 Corinthians 11:23 – 27

It does not appear that we are protected from either the natural consequences of this world nor from the consequences of being Christians. On the contrary persecution and suffering is to be expected and, following Paul, to be boasted about.

The fruit of suffering is also the building of our character. Paul writes of the fruit of suffering being perseverance, character and hope (Romans 5:3). C. S. Lewis put it well : 'suffering is God's anvil on which he purifies our character'. [9] [10] Without suffering there is no refinement, without refinement we cannot come closer to God.

The question that follows is therefore the purpose of prayer. Why pray if, because of man's free will, a fallen creation and God's chosen powerlessness, the prayers of protection we offer cannot be answered? Why pray if, for the above reasons, God cannot intervene in human history? Four types of prayer can be identified in scripture which God is ready, able and willing to answer.

♦ From the model prayer of Jesus we see how God wants us to understand His will in a situation and pray for that.
♦ From prayers such as Daniel's we seen how we are to plead the cause of others, for the sake of God's glory and His name.
♦ Throughout the New Testament Paul emphasises the importance of embracing suffering rather than expecting it to be taken away. By that God's power may be made perfect in weakness. Sometimes God does not ask us to do anything but rather to find ways to be in the face of suffering.
♦ God does ask us to pray in faith for the healing of the sick, for miracles. John 14:12-14 puts it triumphantly. We do not often see the fruit for the reasons outlined above.

Through obedient service we are often the answer to our own prayers. God chooses the humble to bring down the proud. The USA spent untold billions containing the USSR. An electrician in some town in Poland no one had ever heard of said 'enough' and continued to say 'enough' until he became President of Poland and saw the countries to the south of Poland free as well. Corrie Aquino in the Philippines said 'enough' to evil and stood her ground until the evil left. Ghandi said 'enough' to evil from any side, whether British, Hindu or Moslem and fasted[11] until a continent and an empire came round to his way of thinking. Hundreds were massacred in Tiananmen square. The picture that people remember is of a man, armed only with two plastic carrier bags, halting an entire tank column.

The common thread throughout is the willingness to give up everything, even life itself, to combat evil. Solzhenitsyn pointed out that when a man has lost everything he is free to do anything.[12] Christ made the same point. Give up everything, follow me and find freedom. From that freedom will follow the fruits of the kingdom of God and evil will be put to shame – today.

The final piece of the jigsaw puzzle is left until last, probably its rightful place. There is no comment to be made, simply an acknowledgement that we cannot fully understand suffering without conceding the influence of the author of evil. The front cover of Time international in May 1994 carried the caption:

> 'There are no demons left in Hell', the missionary said, 'They are all in Rwanda.'

Interlude 5
The nuns prayed again, as before. Blessing the soldiers, their family, their tribe. Killing with semi automatic weapons is straightforward – all fighters have to do is raise their weapons to waist height and 'spray' their victims. The fighters raised their weapons to waist height.

5. DISPLACEMENT

In chapter 3 I outlined Henri Nouwen's ideas on being displaced from the ordinary and proper place. Part of the dynamic of team life involves being present to one another in shared and common vulnerability. Team members are real to one another both in their giftings and in their weaknesses. Nouwen et al[13] put it more positively: 'Displacement is being called together to make God's compassion visible in the concreteness of everyday living (Acts 2 : 44 – 47)'. It is this aspect which is central to our understanding of the remission of suffering.

The fruit of being displaced from the ordinary and proper place is the phenomenon of an Incarnational lifestyle. By that is meant the idea that those living such a lifestyle reflect Christ to those around them. Our actions are based both on short term, consequential considerations and also on the eternal consequences of our activities. We feed the hungry for a number of reasons. First they are hungry and need food. We are moved by compassion to do something about their hunger simply because it is there. Secondly they are fed because, in so doing, we worship Christ and obey him. The Bible tells us to feed the hungry. Christ went further and said that when we feed the hungry we serve Him not symbolically but directly. In feeding the hungry with the right motivation they are fed not just with food but also with something of the knowledge of Christ. They draw closer to the Christ who is already close to them.

In summary there is a deep richness to the concept of suffering. Perhaps because of the way we have been trained to think analytically in the West we try to understand it aspect by aspect rather than as a whole. In doing so we become trapped by apparently insightful questions which actually do little to illuminate our understanding. As a result we despair that God can act or even exists. The more powerfully we are wedded to the idea of a God who sweeps into our sphere of activity like some comic strip hero to do away with wrong doing, the greater our despair when He apparently fails to appear. Our problem is not that he fails to appear but that we are either looking in the wrong direction or fail to see Christ when He does appear.

In considering suffering we see that God has already borne all our sufferings on the Cross. Indeed He suffers to a greater measure since he chooses to remain true to Himself. The free will that we have been gifted with really is free will and we may choose to worship God as He intended or we may choose evil ways. Where wrong exists we should not always cry 'Satan' but rather ponder the results of the Fall, ponder a God who sees what we see even once we turn away and ponder a God who chooses to work through us. In that He limits Himself since we are free to co-operate or not. However, as we obey Him, we draw closer to Him and see Him in the faces of those we serve. As we serve them, we serve Him and those we serve may draw closer to Him in turn.

The challenge then becomes one of our identity. Are we hid in Christ or are we still 'objects of interest'. Does our identity and response flow from a relationship with a triumphant risen Lord who yet chooses to be powerless so that we may remain free to choose to worship Him and who knows the suffering we see? Further than that 'has got His hands dirty', come down from His throne and suffered alongside us more than we can know? Or do we retain 'our' identity and blame God for the consequences of our actions and those of our fellow humans?

In one part of the world army commanders drive 14 year old boys in front of them. This clears a path through the minefields. In another part of the world a rebel army herds women and children together to starve them. They are produced for the benefit of some aid agencies who bring in food. The army feeds itself as a result and shoots the women and children. Someone sat down in cold blood and designed the gas chambers in Dachau. Someone else sat down in cold blood and designed land mines that maim rather than kill so the victims are more of a drain on enemy resources than a dead body. These are cold blooded choices. These are the consequences of free will given as a good gift to bless us. They are not God's fault. Nor, incidentally, are they necessarily demonic per se. Humans often do a good enough job of evil without the need for Satanic inspiration.

Our compassionate response to suffering involves us in a different sort of exercise of free will. It involves us in responding to the eternal; to Christ, the Cross and Christ-likeness. Christ in turn asks us to be displaced from the ordinary and the proper place and to disappear as an object of interest – not just ridding ourselves of a 'look at me' mentality but being as Christ to those around us. In so doing Christ is made manifest to those who suffer because He too suffers with them and cannot stand their suffering any more than we can.

Coping with Suffering
In practical terms the question often arises of how to cope with suffering,

especially if it has not been directly experienced before. We have to remember that suffering will take a lifetime and then eternity to understand – it is a process. Don't work to figure it all out the first time you see a leper or a dead child or one of the 200 million Christians who live in absolute poverty.

The psychological adjustment is a *process*. In the initial stages of seeing the suffering of others we experience a numbness or shock – what we are experiencing cannot possibly be true. As our senses catch up with reality then anger or fear, depending on our individual way of reacting, will begin. Almost instinctively we will begin a search for something or someone to blame and in the face of overwhelming suffering (a refugee camp for example) can quickly feel helpless. Guilt in its various guises creeps in – 'this is my fault' or, as one aid worker is reported to have said – 'our governments sell the guns to these people. We come in afterwards as the apology'. Doubt about God, our faith, our training, our efficacy is not at all uncommon.

In the midst of all of this we simply get on with the task in front of us. For some we need the big picture and will pursue ways of alleviating suffering at macro level. Others see things at an individual level. 'How do you feed the starving in Africa – the answer is simple, one mouth at a time'.[14] In neither response is doing nothing an option.

Inevitably aid workers and missionaries in the developing world will see horror. The reactions above are to be expected and can be alleviated to some extent by the way in which they set about working through the reactions.

Talk and pray things through with mature people who *understand* exactly what it is you are talking about or keep it to yourself. There is nothing more frustrating than pouring out your feelings to someone who clearly doesn't have the first idea of what you are meaning by your words. If you are surrounded by people who cannot or will not understand then using a diary is absolutely invaluable. In talking to others it is also essential to process and filter what (inevitable) advice you are offered. Job became very adept at this!

In the West we are used to instant everything, including instant answers to our questions. It is better not to look for immediate answers to suffering – sometimes it is enough to express your thoughts and feelings then let them alone for a season.

Take your hard questions to God and wait for some fairly tangential answers! Again there seems to be a process involving dependence on our relationship with God. For reasons that are clear an argument beginning 'God why did you allow this'? is unlikely to get far. Yet, from David's psalms, we see that God is very gracious. He allows us to rage at Him and to have our temper tantrums. As we calm, so it becomes at least possible for him to answer in His still small voice. As has been seen above, however, part of the trick in exploring the issue of suffering is in asking the right questions in the first place.

A man kills children and we dare to ask God why He allowed it when mankinds' only creative contribution to the scene has been the building of the gun. Everything else was made by God and, from Job, we see how we are to approach our creator, sovereign Lord when asking Him these difficult questions. We dare not accuse, we can only approach with reverence to hear His tender reply.

Interlude 6

No-one is entirely sure what happened next. One fighter suddenly had his gun ripped from his hands and thrown some distance down the beach. Yet there was no one visible to do such a thing. The fighters looked at the nuns. 'You're Christians, aren't you'? Before the nuns could reply properly, the fighters ran off, never to return.

[1] Jeffrey Barton Russell quoted in an article by Lance Morrow in an essay on 'Evil', *Time International*, June 10th 1991, p41.
[2] By conciliar decision at Carthage in AD397. The books to be included in the canon of scripture were voted in. Those which nearly made it were victim of the usual committee fudge and became not quite scripture but jolly useful anyway – The Apocrypha.
[3] John Paul II, *Crossing the Threshold of Hope*, London, Jonathan Cape, 1994.
[4] Pinnock, C., et al *Openness to God*, Carlisle, IVP, 1994.
[5] Forster, R.T., and Marston, V.P., *Gods Strategy in Human History*, Crowborough, Highland Books, 1989.
[6] Pinnock, C., et al *Openness to God*, Carlisle, IVP, 1994.
[7] Ware, T., *The Orthodox Way*, London, Penguin, 1979.
[8] Priestland, G., *Who Needs the Church?* Edinburgh, St Andrews Press, 1983.
[9] Quoted in 'Shadowlands'.
[10] Light relief at this point. YWAMers are very into character forming events in their lives. A Calvinist, an Arminian and a YWAMer died and went to hell. The Calvinist ascribed this to God's choice, the Arminian to some forgotten choice she had made. The YWAMer looked round thoughtfully. 'I wonder what God is trying to teach me in this situation?'.
[11] NB – 'fasted' not 'hunger strike' which comes from a quite different mentality.
[12] Solzhenitsyn, A., *The First Circle*, Harmondsworth, Penguin, 1968 Ch 17.
[13] Nouwen et al, op cit, Chapter 5.
[14] Dr Gary Parker, chief surgeon on YWAM's ship The Anastasis, during a YWAM conference at Le Rucher, France, 1996.

Appendix 1

Sample routine re-entry simulations for training debriefers

Simulations are fairly straightforward to generate provided they are done from the perspective of the underlying dynamics to be simulated. They should never be generated from the perspective of a difficult personal experience or the motivation of 'let's see what they make of this difficult/nasty/horrible situation'. The purpose of training debriefers is to get them into a way of thinking which will help them access the almost universal processes that people go through on re-entry and to build their confidence in dealing with the 90% of debriefing scenarios they will come across and help to resolve successfully. The 10% of situations they can't handle can be referred on – this is not the place to give them advanced training in counselling.

Each of the following scenarios is therefore built around the common dynamics outlined in Chapter 3 – Isolation, guilt at leaving, guilt at being home, God, health etc.

For the purpose of this training it seems best to have a group of about 6 people playing the part of returnees, one person doing the debriefing and a trainer to comment and to help out if people get stuck. The aim is to identify the underlying dynamics. Encourage the 'returnees' to co-operate with the process and to stick to their script.

Each scenario can take between 20 minutes and all day to work through depending on the size and garrulousness of the group. We normally schedule a maximum of an hour per scenario. Remember you want everyone who is being trained to have at least two practice runs at conducting a debriefing session.

The following are sample simulations which can be copied for each 'returnee'. It's fine that they all have the same script, they'll interpret it in different ways. It is best to keep things simple at this level of training. The purpose is for the debriefing trainees to grow in confidence and skill at identifying core dynamics from people's stories.

Simulation 1

You thoroughly enjoyed the team and felt very at home. You are now back in a small unfriendly department at work and living with one other flatmate. The people at the church you attend have asked many questions about the weather, the food whilst away and so on but little about the work. You are also increasingly disturbed by the glib way in which very dear friends of yours live their lives – they don't understand what the world is really like. You would like to join any agency now to get back to the exciting existence you had abroad. Going to supermarkets and similar places makes you feel cross but you aren't sure why.

Simulation 2

Home after ten years of being away is not like coming home at all. You don't feel at home here, strangely you now realise you never felt truly 'at home' abroad either. You feel life has passed you by – computers, films, shows, TV seems odd and difficult to get to grips with. You are now significantly older with lots of accomplishments but none which are of value back here. All your friends have also moved on in their lives and you have little truly in common with them. Perhaps coming off the field was a mistake – where do you fit? You feel cut off, with no one who can really understand how torn you feel about responding to God's call to return home, yet leaving so much behind.

Simulation 3

Your time away was good from a team point of view but very little was accomplished due to unexpected floods. Your church and supporters want to know why more didn't get done and you feel quite pressured by them and quite misunderstood. You did accomplish a lot in prayer and the local people were grateful you came. You were clear God asked you to go but don't understand why He asked you to go at a time when you could not accomplish anything very concrete. Life since your return has been trying – people are so caught up with *things*. It is so easy to accomplish things and you can't stop thinking about those you left behind, what they are doing. You feel bad about being home, angry at the complacency of the west and a little uncertain for the first time about God's goodness.

Simulation 4

The year was great, by and large, wonderful team and excellent training. The cholera outbreak which killed so many in the orphanage quite needlessly has left you very sad – you frequently find yourself crying for no obvious reason and feel helpless about what happened. God was gracious in spearing so many and clearly spoke into many people's lives during that time. The Church at home has been wonderful and have given you a lot of space to work things through. You feel OK about the future and are looking forward to getting on with life. You want to put the whole experience behind you, forget it and move on. You are in two minds as to what to say today in case things get stirred up needlessly.

Appendix 2

Training Simulators

Training simulators are designed to mimic particular dynamics or situations that course participants are being trained for. The best thing to do is to make up your own tailored to the particular course or field location you are training and the issues that are likely to be faced. The stages are:

1. Deciding the issues to be faced and experienced.

2. Designing a string of situations to simulate those situations.

3. Material preparation.

4. Staff briefing and rehearsal if necessary.

5. The simulator.

6. Debriefing of the students as a large group.

1. Typical issues that can be simulated using an airport style scenario:
   i) relationship before task – we have 'airport staff' break from duties for a chat with friends about family etc.
   ii) low priority on time – 'airport staff' move slowly and at a comfortable rate.
   iii) need for group decision making / responsibility – have (typically) customs officers or immigration officers etc. break off for lengthy consultations with their superiors.
   iv) Beggars/con men at airports. Make use of 'Missionary Kids' if possible – they seem extraordinarily good at begging. Use some of your smooth talking staff to persuade (gullible) participants to part with money, baggage or to take parcels through customs or to change money. Have the various cons prepared (swapping dollars for money wrapped in tissue paper, parcels with (fake!) drugs in them and so on).
   v) Canadians often seem popular abroad because of their perceived neutrality, other nationalities less so for either historical reasons or current perceived cultural imperialism, e.g. Brits, Yanks and Germans. Have immigration differentially give the various nationalities a hard time as a function of the country being visited (e.g. Brits get a hard time in India and some parts of E. Africa, Americans in Europe and some parts of the far East and so on).

It's important for staff to give the participants a hard time for a clear purpose – it is easy for the game to drift into 'rude staff' or giving students a hard time simply to stress them and 'see how they do'. Stressing the students for the sake of it is not enough. For that reason the staff briefing is crucial and, wherever possible, using staff who have travelled abroad and been through the situations they are mimicking.

2. The scenario can then be designed – e.g. airport, border crossing, getting a visa, obtaining permission to stay in country, exiting the country or any other routine encounter with officialdom from a different culture. Note this is *not* an exercise to train them how to get through a concrete situation such as an airport but rather an opportunity to expose them to a different and culturally valid way of doing things.

3. Material preparation – things we've found helpful are:

money (photocopied dollar bills for example)
imitation passport
health certificate
signs – 'Immigration' etc., 'closed', 'Office'
different clothing for officials
asking the students to pack a bag – it is handed in and then (eventually) claimed at baggage handling. Some goes missing. Most bags are searched (we've found from experience it's less embarrassing for the *staff* (!) to have men search mens bags and vice versa). *Anything* suspicious gets the security police's attention (cameras for example). Periodically customs ask if a participant 'has anything for them or their family'.
A large room or several rooms attached. Participants who make it through should go somewhere out the way.

We let the simulation go for about 60 minutes. Some students will be through in 20 minutes – others won't have made it.

4. Briefing. We find it best to give the staff written briefing and at least 5-7 minutes to set up their 'stalls'. Remind them of the purpose of the exercise and, whilst in role, to keep observing how the students are doing.

5. Have fun!

6. Allow about 15 – 30 minutes for debriefing the exercise. Think of the issues that came up and draw participants *reactions* out. Did the participants look after each other or just press on independently? What were staffs' observations?

NB some participants, particularly those who have not travelled at all, can be very upset by the exercise, not so much because they experience 'rudeness' or 'frustration' but the sudden fear that they may not be cut out for mission. Some, indeed, may not be!

Set out below is an example of an 'airport' simulation although the actual location is less relevant than the dynamics involved.

2 teams of participants.

4 staff:

Nurse, baggage claim, immigration, customs.

Large room with 2 exits – **30 minutes to set up.** 30 – 50 minutes to complete. 10 minutes to debrief.

4 desks

Nurse at entry point
Needs to see Health certificate. Insist, at random, on 2 or 3 people having:
Either an AIDS test (it's the regulations)
or Yellow Fever jab (their certificate is not in order).

Watch:
Do the rest of their team stay behind to support them?

Does the victim:
protest effectively?
attempt to bribe their way out of trouble?
insist on the AIDS kit being used?

Material
AIDS kit per team
Health certificate per team member

Baggage claim
At a convenient break in the schedule participants bring a *bag labelled with their name, address and team destination.*

Before starting the simulation participants are given a baggage claim which matches up with their bag.

One bag from each team is lost but (much later) found.

Baggage handler – slowly – matches up baggage claim to bag.
Also suggests that people give 'small small' for getting bag.
Also takes frequent breaks to chat to other staff.

Watch – does team stick together and support each other?
   – do teams give 'small small'?

Immigration
Careful inspection of every passport – and photograph.
Ask for address in country.
Fill out immigration form.
Ask for 1 in 4 passports back 'for further checks'.
For one or two passports the Immigration officer should disappear from sight altogether.

Watch : do students stay calm and courteous?
Do they give accurate yet sensitive answers?

Customs
Careful search of every other bag.
Officious questioning.
Careful examination of all literature.
Frequent consultation with Immigration Officer.

Watch : do students stay calm and courteous?
Do they give accurate yet sensitive answers?

Appendix 3

Pastoral Visits

Pastoral visits to overseas teams can be invaluable if done well. There is increasing clarity as to what constitutes a good visit but no rigorous research into their efficacy.[1]

There is a trade off with any visits between supporting the people on the field and getting in the way. Thus for any pastoral visit there needs to be a clear aim and a clear time limit. Aims can include supporting the individual missionaries or workers, helping to evaluate the work itself and offering a wider analysis not just of the individual project but also the context in which that project is happening.

Pastoral visits can also be made in times of crisis, e.g. for critical incident debriefing or to provide outside consultancy for team issues such as conflict. Pastoral visits are seen as essential for students on practical placements following a course.

Students

Placements can vary from a few months to several years depending on the nature of the course. The following reflects the thinking behind a typical placement visit to students led by trainee leaders on a three month placement. The principles can be extrapolated to other forms of outreach.

There are three areas of concern for the visitor. The first is the wellbeing of the team members – are they learning the things they should? Are they doing well in themselves? Are there any problematic team dynamics and so on? The second is the interaction of the team as a whole with the local situation – how are they integrating with the local people? With other missionaries? With the local programme? With other agencies including the local church? The final consideration is the nature of the locality – is it intrinsically a satisfactory placement which can be approached for future placements?

The pastoral visit is made by senior leadership staff who have the authority to take whatever action necessary to change a situation should it be required. The visit is made during the middle week of the field placement with one weeks' flexibility allowed either way. The duration of the visit is reckoned at one day on site per team member with a minimum of three days on site and a maximum stay of eight or nine days. Any less is inadequate to complete the agenda of the pastoral visit, any more means that the senior leadership begin to get in the way of any trainee leader's authority or of the long term dynamics of the team.

Each team member is seen individually (and in private) and time is given to talk about their personal reactions to outreach, what they are learning and their immediate goals for the rest of their outreach. Team leaders are also seen in private, principally to talk through the same agenda. Talking about the individual team members beyond some global comments is usually unnecessary. The project and their perceptions of how they are integrating with the local situation are talked through.

Input is given both to team leaders and to group members to help them to see things in perspective, whether good or bad.

An extended time is spent with local leadership who may be the overall project managers or project owners, other agency staff and, where possible, time is also spent with beneficiaries. The aim of the conversations is for the visitors to assess both how well the team is serving the local project objectives and also how well the local project is serving the team's learning objectives both in principal and in reality. During this time there will often be negotiations both for future teams and also approaches made regarding the possibility of recruiting particular students from the current placement. Inevitably the visitors will become caught up in many other activities as would be anticipated.

The anecdotal value of these visits is incalculable. Teams visited look forward to their mail, to outside news, to a chance to take stock and a chance to talk to other staff who know them well. Many field leaders are grateful for the chance to negotiate future teams and for training staff to see the location for themselves and hence be better equipped to form and prepare teams for future placements.

The overwhelming majority of student placements go well or very well and the pastoral visit acts very much as an encouragement and a chance to take stock. On occasion however the visitor may well be asked to become involved in difficult situations, usually conflict resolution, sometimes time-tabling difficulties and sometimes with individuals who are clearly unable to cope with the challenges of overseas work.

Pastoral visits for field staff

For long term staff other forms of pastoral visit become available and these are inevitably less structured. The agenda can remain much the same although the visitors can be very different. It is, for example, particularly encouraging that supporting churches feel increasingly able to send people to visit individual people on the field and simply to come alongside them with a deep interest in them as people and also in the work they are doing.

Visits to a team in response to a particular crisis are perhaps the most difficult debriefing task to accomplish. The crisis can be an acute one such as a critical incident or a chronic situation which has come to a head, such as team disunity or outright hostility. Critical incidents are dealt with elsewhere. The issue of a more deep-seated problem which comes to a head can be dealt with here.

In dealing with the problem in a Christian setting it is necessary to check several things. First and foremost checking that the reconciliation services that are available locally have truly been exhausted is vital. The second is identifying clearly who is making the request for outside help. In some instances it can be outside management in which case the local team may or may not have truly bought in to the idea of an outsider arriving to 'sort things out'. In some cases it may be the local team who has asked for a pastoral visit in which case the visitor needs to ensure that they have the necessary authority and scope to act as the need arises. I have been caught out both ways. Usually where management have been the instigators the outsider can manage to 'join' the team and do some useful work.

More tricky is the case where the team insists on outside help but without giving the visitor the appropriate scope for action. A common situation that I have been involved in a number of times is where an individual member of a team simply does not fit with the team as a whole and yet is indispensable to that team. In spending time with the team things may well improve but the improvement is often transitory and due more to an outsider reducing the pressure than effecting lasting change. In team dynamic terms the problem actually is insoluble and the person who does not fit should withdraw. Management may be reluctant to see things that way because the team member is vital to the project and so the team member stays.

Part of the solution for the pastoral visitor is a written brief in advance which is prepared and signed both by the field leader and by the relevant headquarters manager. The brief should make clear the pastoral visitor's authority and scope for action.

In all pastoral visits a key consideration is that of credibility. A visitor is unlikely to be able to support field workers unless at least one of the following is true:

- a pre-existing good relationship with team members
- good working knowledge of the project
- good working knowledge and experience of the local culture including language.

If none of the above are true then the pastoral visit is more likely to be a hindrance than a help.

---

[1] Frances White in O'Donnell 1992 op cit has outlined some helpful guidelines for field consultants in general which are also relevant to those conducting pastoral visits.

Appendix 4

Career interviews

There is a scarcity of professionally trained personnel managers and occupational psychology trained managers throughout missions and, possibly, throughout aid work. The basic requirements of matching people to task-analysed jobs using valid and reliable selection procedures are often missing with the result that people can end up significantly underachieving or significantly stressed because they are competent people in the wrong job. Furthermore agencies may fail to follow through on people to ensure they are pursuing an adequate career track.

There is a constant tension for staff in larger missions between the Christian ideal of being a servant and pursuing one's call; between filling the staffing need and fulfilling the requirements of one's own job. For so called 'faith missions' where recruitment to 'support roles' such as housekeeping or clerical work is often problematic this can lead to inefficiency and frustration.

The classic example is that of cooking for relatively large numbers of people. Cooking for 50 or more people is not domestic cooking on a larger scale but an entirely different approach with, in many countries, a plethora of legal and professional obligations. It can be done by amateurs but the inefficiency is noticeable as is the quality of the product. Yet often willing or not so willing volunteers are obliged to fill this type of gap so that the ministry can continue.

In facing these issues one can either wait for a cohort of appropriately trained personnel managers to arrive or find some simple solutions to each of the issues that do arise. Selection and other topics have been covered in the main body of the book. Outside of that is establishing quality control mechanisms to ensure that 'employees' of missions and aid agencies are doing the right job in the right place for the right length of time which both maximises the employees' effectiveness and also their job satisfaction.

One principle and one technique are described here. The principle is straightforward and is the absolute commitment of 'managers' to use only appropriately qualified people for the tasks they are responsible for. On rare and exceptional circumstances this will not always be possible. The YWAM base where I live was once hit by a serious outbreak of food poisoning. Of some 60 staff at the time seven made it to work the following day, 3 left hurriedly after an hour. It was left to the remainder of very junior staff to run the base, staff reception, check logistics such as heating and nurse the ill. It is this order of rarity I am outlining.

The domino effect of simply plugging staffing gaps with whoever is around can be startling with, after a few months or a year, no one doing anything effectively and the community experiencing a sense of permanent crisis. Staffing the gaps, except in extremis, can also be the most effective way of turning a deaf ear to what God may be saying through the circumstances. Often the cry is heard 'we must keep this ministry going'. Well, who says so? Why does 'my' agency have to do this work? Why does this work 'have' to continue? Who, if anyone, knows where the 'off' button is to a ministry, i.e. how to judge when the ministries' task is either complete or redundant?

The technique that is used throughout much of YWAM England to establish the career goals of future staff is the 'three interview' system. This was established by Laurence Singlehurst and Steven Sullivan, respectively the YWAM national director for England and the DTS director for the UK to meet the challenge of very low recruitment results from the Discipleship Training Schools that were being run and which provide all future YWAM staff. Several theories existed as to why this was the case but close examination revealed that students and, to a large extent, staff were ignorant of career opportunities in YWAM or other agencies. Students, where placed, responded to specific, concrete job opportunities which matched their skills and calling. However placement rates were often running at 10% or fewer with one infamous DTS failing to place any students at all out of a class of thirty.

For YWAM readers or for people from similar training agencies there have been a number of developments to turn those figures around. (For agency personnel interested purely in career guidance, the following paragraphs can safely be skipped). It quickly became apparent that several things needed to be in place for career guidance to work adequately. YWAM(England) in particular took something of a detour during the late 1970's and early 1980's and began to recruit numbers of DTS students who were in need of counselling. A discipleship programme was seen as the way forward both by churches and by YWAM itself and the DTS programme, for many, but not all students, became a counselling clinic. This attitude had to be turned round and, by and large, DTS leaders are now wedded to the idea that a DTS is a missions training programme for, basically, whole and healthy individuals.

Some DTS programmes have taken this a stage further and have minimum selection criteria and a broad target range (e.g. 70%) of students from each DTS that they expect to be placed in missions within a specified period. Such criteria are seen as guidelines not rules but they give selectors and school staff a sense of containment and guidance as to what they are aiming for. However the DTS programme is not a sausage factory churning out missionaries, it is a chance for people to meet with God in a radical way and, from that place, determine their future course.

The outcome reflected above has been the subject of debate. Demographically the pool of Western young people available to mission is shrinking and this may not feel like the time to become picky or directive. Those adopting the approach outlined here however have been interested to note that both the number and the quality of applications has risen each year. The approach above demonstrates a commitment to excellence, the result is excellent students all of whom have a call to mission and who simply need placing.

Career Interviews

A three step interview process is used for YWAM DTS students. A modified 'management by objectives' approach has also been used for some YWAM staff.

Three interviews are conducted with each student by a senior member of the school staff and the student's small group leader.

The purpose of the first interview is simply to see how the student is doing on the course after the first few weeks. Usually, by this stage, students have determined whether the approach of YWAM is for them.[1] If it is not then this is a good time to leave, little is lost on either side and it frees both student and staff to move on. Further background information is gathered about the student, in particular their function calling (i.e. the ministry or profession they are called to, e.g. evangelism with prostitutes, relief work, civil engineering, etc.) and/or their country or people calling. Other information can also be gleaned. For many professional students their career history is useful and can give a feel for how long they tend to stay in a particular job and how their skills have related to their work so far.

Staff and student need to explore quite candidly the type of agency the student is best suited to. For some the fuzzy, open, fluid, entrepreneurial spirit of agencies such as YWAM is a pleasurable challenge. They have the freedom to develop and are not, in their perception, throttled. For others the system is too fluid and they prefer structure imposed or constructed by others. For some a 'faith mission' is too much to contemplate; a salary, or at least an allowance is necessary and so on. The interviewers are thus teasing out from the student the extent to which they can flourish in an agency such as YWAM once they leave the contained structure and atmosphere of a training course.

At this stage further information may be superfluous, the aim is to put the student in contact with potential 'employers' not to interview the students for those jobs.

From the interview information plus the information on file, school staff generate a very short list of potential jobs at a second, brief, interview. Experience has shown that three – four job suggestions seem to be the optimum number to offer. Many more suggestions becomes overwhelming and the student tends to become paralysed, unable to choose between the various options and, often trapped by feeling that they need to find the absolute right job.

Staff then work on the students behalf to get information, application forms and contact numbers for the students. (This is not seen as infantalising the students, the work described is purely clerical, involving e-mail, international faxes and so forth and students usually have better things to do with their time). Applications are made and, in theory, processed whilst students are away on outreach. The third interview is then held during their debriefing week to monitor progress and ensure that students have concrete plans and strategies for the time following the course.

Staff interviews

Elsewhere in YWAM a modified form of 'management by objectives' is used. Five sets of information are gained from the staff member prior to joining a department:

education and work history
perceived strengths and areas to develop (not weaknesses)
perceived likes and dislikes related to 'work'
any relevant personality assessments (e.g. Myers Briggs)
current or long term words from the Lord

From this list a range of conclusions can be generated.

The educational background will give some indication as to the minimum level at which the person would be expected to function. It is always worth asking whether the candidate got as far as they wanted to with their studies and to be open to them completing those studies either within work time or to take time out to complete them.

Work history will give an indication of the extent to which the person has progressed or been side-tracked and some indication of their preferred length of service. Usually problems or potential problems are glaringly obvious both to the interviewer and the interviewee. One nurse was amazed to realise she had not stayed in one job, with one exception, for longer than six months and had spent much of her career outside her chosen profession. She perceived herself as wanting to stay put for several years at a time and she has engineered things accordingly since then. Another candidate had been with one company for twenty years, the transition to a loosely organised agency was difficult and she returned to a more stable situation.

The candidates strengths and areas to develop are vital to explore. We refuse to ask about weaknesses with respect to work since we are not recruiting their weaknesses nor will their weaknesses be managed. The list is also checked against their likes and dislikes. A common area of tension frequently emerges between a candidates strength which also happens to be an area of dislike. Many candidates, for example, are good at administration but actively dislike it. Yet agencies are often desperate for administrative support and so place the person in that slot. The person leaves, goes sick or burns out quickly in such a situation.

Personality tests, when understood properly, have a vital part to play. The details of office layout, to take a simple example, can be influenced by people's personality. For an introvert an open plan office can be murder with the constant interruptions. For an extrovert a private office can be excruciating. Some people are at their most creative in a team setting, others work best individually and then bring their ideas for consideration when well formed. Some people prefer contained, well formed, time limited projects to work on, others prefer global, fluid, open ended commitments. Trying to force the wrong personality type into a job, no matter how well qualified they are apart from personality, will simply cause misery.

Finally, considerable weight needs to be given to what the person understands God to be saying to them. Some people do need time out to hear what God is saying and so take time to work in an area with less responsibility than they are used to for a season. Others are being encouraged to branch out, take courage, try new things and so on. The job again, needs to match these vital indications.

From this an outline ideal job description can be generated for the person together with personal goals for the coming year in terms of development. The task of the manager then becomes one of melding the ministry aims with the strengths and calling of their staff member and then stepping back out of the way whilst they take off. Alternatively the manger can, genuinely, let the person go so they can move on into the ministry God has for them outside their current department or ministry. God loves a cheerful giver!

The time involved in such career guidance varies from person to person. Generally, the very first time such a process is gone through, anything up to four or five hours work can be expected. The second and subsequent times involve considerably less time, perhaps ninety minutes or so per year for a major review and further meetings during the year to monitor progress.

---

[1] For students who are on the wrong track but still stumble on, the rule of thumb measurement I have suggested is quantity of time taken up by a student in staff meetings. If more than one hour per week is devoted to discussing the student then they are either in the wrong place entirely or, if they are in the right place, changes need to happen quickly, say within a week.

Appendix 5

Missionary Kids

The following section, written in note form, relies heavily on a presentation given at Bawtry Hall in June 1996 during a conference on debriefing.

A key issue in thinking about the preparation of children is less preparation of the children and more selection and preparation of families.

The majority of MKs are adjusted, many are not. So – do we not send families? If we do send them how do we do it well?

Opportunities for preparation of families by missions:

The preparation for families begins with the application process which can show that the agency cares about the children. It can also provide important information to the family that the agency has thought through the logistics and emotional issue surrounding families moving overseas.

The interview stage may need to consider including the children at an appropriate age to ascertain their ability to cope with an overseas move.

The orientation phase can be a disorienting phase for children, particularly younger ones. They may see little of their parents during a time when, clearly, change is in the air. The agency may spend little time with the children, particularly teenagers, to give them the same cross cultural orientation and briefing that their parents are receiving.

Africa Inland Mission run a 5 day orientation (mornings only) which contains bible stories, cultural points, health, language and emotional issues of relevance to the child such as what they are leaving behind (pets, friends etc). In the USA Linkcare have a 5 week programme in parallel with their adult programme. The message throughout is one of parents and children being in this together.

Ten key pieces of information were identified that it was felt missionary families needed to know in relationship to their training. The information given below is presented at an experiential level but it is possible to validate some of the insights along the way with our knowledge of developmental psychology and family dynamics.

Loving families (defined as ones where the parents were able to show affection to each other in front of children) make strong MKs although the reverse is not necessarily true. It is interesting that the issue of cohesion as in the ability to give and receive affection is raised again in the context of a family but not surprising if one thinks of a family as a team.

Not too surprisingly the second point reflects the need for consultative leadership from the adults in the family. This dynamic is translated into the need to explain things to children according to their age.

The age bands cannot be exact but roughly under age three the children need simply to be told. At this age a child's sense of confidence and security is very much a function of parental confidence and security. Broadly speaking if the parents are secure in the move then infants will also be secure. Between the ages of three and five the children are still informed of the move but given more extensive information, for example pictures or videos of where they are to move to and the sorts of things they can expect to see and do.

Beyond six the children need to be increasingly involved in the decision making so that they feel included and a part of the process. However it is important that the children do not take the responsibility for the decisions onto themselves. That responsibility can only lie with the adults in the family.

Beyond twelve the advice is simple – do not take a reluctant child.

The third piece of advice is "Never say 'never'" It is entirely possible, in fact inevitable, that parents will change their mind about key things affecting children, for example, boarding school, home schooling, going away for trips and so on.

You and your children don't have to be perfect. Children are very forgiving of family faults and problems. What they find difficult to cope with is secrets and hypocrisy. For the younger child morals and principles are very clear cut and their thinking tends to be very conservative. For parents to try to pretend in public to be other than they truly are is difficult for the child to understand. Continually to be living up to impossibly high standards can lead to problems not just during childhood but also later in life.

Plan ahead for key events in the children's life – a child, in the non derogatory sense is ego centric. That is, an event of importance to them, such as a birthday or a school play is, de facto, of importance to their parents and friends.

It's OK to take a holiday. This is not so much a message for families as for missionaries in general. The perceived pressures of missionary life can often leave all those involved believing themselves to be indispensable, or believing that the task is too important to leave or feeling guilty at the location of the logical location for their holiday.

Encourage celebration of birthdays, anniversaries, friends, anything and everything. As a family enjoy the chance to keep old family traditions and to make new traditions. Edith Schaeffer is quoted as saying that 'memories are worth buying'.

Take time to say goodbyes to both the adult's friends as well as to the children's friends.

You and your kids are on the same side. Children are generally very loyal to their parents and feel strongly that if things are going wrong then somehow it is their own fault. Again communication is crucial both in the good times and the not so good times. To the extent that individual children have the capacity to understand they will be reassured by their parents openness with them and will not feel the pressure of some secret, which they may be to blame for, being withheld from them.

You are coming back. It is helpful for the children to retain as much as possible of their heritage – family and national – as is possible given their age. That way the feeling of coming to a foreign place is at least partially diminished.

When such a process goes well the result is a joy to see. I remember meeting a teenage son of a German missionary serving in Spain with an American agency. The son was fluent in three languages and a vibrant Christian. Yet his personality went far beyond anything I had ever seen before – when he spoke Spanish he became Spanish, when speaking German his persona changed again. For his English he was the all American kid. He was at home in many different cultures, well travelled already and confident that his identity did not come from anything so trivial as his background.

Appendix 6

The Main Recommendations of the Macnair Report 1995

SELECTION AND RECRUITMENT
- All candidates participate in a rigorous selection procedure
- Candidates are screened for vulnerability factors
- Effective registers of suitable, qualified, available personnel are maintained
- Appropriate methods are used to identify and short-list eligible candidates for posts
- Field staff are recruited against specific job descriptions

BRIEFING AND TRAINING
- Induction and briefing programmes are provided for all newly arrived field staff
- Comprehensive briefing programmes are provided prior to departure when appropriate
- Security briefing and training are provided prior to departure when appropriate
- Appropriate training for field staff is provided including stress management techniques, negotiating skills and conflict resolution
- Management training for staff is provided on an ongoing basis

MANAGEMENT ON THE FIELD
- Strategies for maintaining continuity in the field are developed
- Strategies are developed to reduce stress in the field
- Appropriate and timely security guidelines for field conditions are developed
- Strategies are developed for dealing with risk taking behaviour
- Performance review procedures are developed and implemented

DEBRIEFING AND SUPPORT
- Appropriate professional debriefing mechanisms are developed
- Methods are developed to improve the use of field information to monitor and evaluate programmes

- Methods are developed to ensure the psychological health of field workers

TERMS AND CONDITIONS
- Adequate health care is provided for field workers
- Adequate insurance cover is provided for all field workers
- Agencies implement disciplinary and grievance procedures for staff

Appendix 7

People In Aid Statement of Principles[1]

Principle 1

THE PEOPLE WHO WORK FOR US ARE INTEGRAL TO OUR EFFECTIVENESS AND SUCCESS

Our approach to people who work in our organisation is a fundamental part of our work. We recognise that the effectiveness and success of our organisation depends on all the people who work for us. Human resource issues are integral to our strategic plans.

Principle 2

OUR HUMAN RESOURCE POLICIES AIM FOR BEST PRACTICE

We recognise that our human resource policies should constantly aim for best practice. We do not aim to respond solely to minimum legal, professional or donor requirements.

Principle 3

OUR HUMAN RESOURCE POLICIES AIM TO BE EFFECTIVE, EFFICIENT, FAIR AND TRANSPARENT

We recognise that our policies must enable us to achieve both effectiveness in our work and good quality of working life for our staff. Our human resource policies therefore aim to be effective, efficient, fair and transparent and to promote equality of opportunity.

Principle 4

WE CONSULT OUR FIELD STAFF WHEN WE DEVELOP HUMAN RESOURCE POLICY

We recognise that we must implement, monitor and continuously develop our human resource policies in consultation with the people who work for us. We aim to include field personnel in our process, whether they are full time, part time, temporary, short term or long term members of our staff.

Principle 5

PLANS AND BUDGETS REFLECT OUR RESPONSIBILITIES TOWARDS OUR FIELD STAFF

We recognise that the effectiveness and success of our field operations depend on the contribution of all the salaried, contract or volunteer staff involved in them. Operational plans and budgets aim to reflect fully our responsibilities for staff management support, development, security and well being.

Principle 6

WE PROVIDE APPROPRIATE TRAINING AND SUPPORT

We recognise that we must provide relevant training and support to help staff work effectively and professionally. We aim to give them appropriate personal and professional support and development before, during and after their field assignments.

Principle 7

WE TAKE ALL REASONABLE STEPS TO ENSURE STAFF SECURITY AND WELL BEING

We recognise that the work of relief and development agencies often places great demands on staff in conditions of complexity and risk. We take all reasonable steps to ensure the security and well-being of staff and their families.

---

[1] The People In Aid Code of Best Practice, RRN Paper 20 Overseas Development Institute, London, 1997.